W9-BTJ-327

Alfred E. Smith as Governor of New York. (Museum of the City of New York)

A Catholic Runs for President

THE CAMPAIGN OF 1928

By

EDMUND A. MOORE

GLOUCESTER, MASS.
PETER SMITH
1968

Library of Congress Catalog Card Number: 56-10167

PRINTED IN THE UNITED STATES OF AMERICA

For

Frances

Preface

This is a study of a brief but important phase of a problem very old in American history. Anti-Catholicism was brought to these shores by early settlers. The fear and hostility that created it, like Catholic antipathy for Protestantism, was a legacy of the sixteenth century. Anti-Romanism was rampant in the mid-nineteenth century, shortly before the Civil War. Despite occasional reappearances of the malady, it seemed improbable that it was destined for a revival in the twentieth century. Yet the third decade of the present century saw so great a resurgence of the old fear that a haunting suspicion lingers that anti-Catholicism may now be no more than dormant.

This book has its setting in a brief time-space not long after the Progressive movement reached its culmination. It was assumed that large-scale movements directed against Catholics belonged to the past. But so old an emotion as "No-Popery" proved responsive to a favorable climate. The nineteen twenties were such a time; the decade witnessed a freshening of the tree of bigotry and a harvest of bitter fruit. This demonstration of the vitality of the old hate came as a distinct shock to many Americans.

In 1918 Alfred E. Smith, a Catholic, became Governor of New York. Defeated in 1920 because of a tremendous tidal wave of Republicanism, two years later he resumed his governorship creating a remarkable four-term record of executive leadership in modernizing the Empire State.

On the national scene the departure from the pattern of Progressivism was well under way before the Democrats left office in 1921. In Wilson's second term, war needs and postwar frustrations combined to end further domestic reform. After 1920 the crusade to prevent war was in abeyance. At this point voters turned to the Grand Old Party of Harrison and McKinley, as well as Lincoln, to preside over a decade of prosperity and indifference. It was a dismal time for the opposition. But by the mid-twenties, the Democrats had in Al Smith a leader with many of the attributes of the authentic American hero.

The New York Governor was a product of the new urban frontier. His beginnings were humble. His early income came from the Fulton fish market; his political education came from all that was available, Tammany Hall. His formal education was not extensive, but he early displayed a great gift for histrionics and an even greater one for politics. His ability to master complicated detail and explain it in simple terms has been matched by few statesmen. Applying it to the political art, he won the admiration of its leading practitioners as well as its academic professors. Only the ill-informed, the prejudiced, and those who made a fetish of the outward trappings of learning, presumed to deny Smith's political genius.

Smith had a magic hold on the affections of the people. Many leaders of the Republican party in New York frankly acknowledged the brilliance of his mind and the solid quality of his constructive record. In a bleak decade for the Democratic party, Al Smith was a hero type with the attraction, at least for urban Americans, of an Andrew Jackson.

Smith's presidential star rose in a period of Republican prosperity, of Prohibition still firmly backed by millions of sincere people, and of resurgent nativism. Successful in winning his party's nomination in 1928, his chances for the presidency were greatly reduced by the undeniable fact of urban prosperity. Opposition to the placing of sumptuary legislation in the Constitution did not become a winning issue for the Democrats until the Great Depression had changed men's outlooks. The Eighteenth Amendment was still sacrosanct and still a formidable roadblock in the path of any candidate opposed to Prohibition. To millions of evangelical Protestants it was a *de facto* point of religious orthodoxy that seemed to eclipse all other reforms and to transcend all other issues.

Of the two problems, Prohibition and religious bigotry, the former is the more easily comprehended. Part of the explanation is that religion was the "silent issue." To discuss it was felt to be bad manners and poor politics. But it cannot be ignored by the historian, one of whose aims is to throw light on the dark and neglected parts of the human story. This book presents an evaluation of the part played by the religious issue insofar as it is possible to isolate it from other issues.

Use in this book of the word "religion" is subject to valid objections. If there were a serviceable substitute it would be used. Since there is none, the word will serve, and without the encumbrance of quotation marks. Religion may well refer, under differing circumstances, to faith, doctrine, ritual, or to church government. The reader should apply the meaning, or the combination of meanings, that the particular phase suggests as most apposite.

The book makes considerable use of direct quotations. This permits the retention of the original tone and color. Another and related advantage may be even more important. The subject is delicate. Certainly it is exceptionally controversial. It lends itself easily to misinterpretation. The writer has attempted through the sources to give the reader a balanced picture of an important chapter in recent history. Much of it is unpleasant to recall. But it is important because it is relevant to the struggle to achieve full political equality for all citizens, to the degree that their capacities of mind and heart allow.

I should like to thank the members of the staffs of the libraries of the University of Connecticut, the State Library at Hartford, the State Library at Albany, the Franklin D. Roosevelt Library, the Hartford Theological Seminary, the Union Theological Seminary, the Catholic University of America, the Manuscripts Division of the Library of Congress, the University of Virginia, Duke University, the University of North Carolina, and the Museum of the City of New York for their kind cooperation.

I am indebted to the administration of the University of Connecticut for twice reducing my teaching assignments—without this it would have been impossible for me to complete the book. I wish to thank my friend and colleague André Schenker for the recent sharing of many of my administrative duties, and my other colleagues at the University of Connecticut who have so generously helped me.

I am grateful for the time given me by Mr. Bernard M. Baruch, Mr. James A. Farley, Mr. Arthur Krock, Mr. Walter Lippmann, Mr. James J. Mahoney, Judge Joseph M. Proskauer, Mr. Ellery Sedgwick, and Mr. Herbert Bayard Swope, as well as Governor Smith's daughter, Mrs. John A. Warner. Their advice and recollections contributed much.

I wish to thank the Social Science Research Council for two grants-in-aid to help defray some of the cost of traveling and photostating.

At a low point of the enterprise Dr. Annarie P. Cazel was very helpful; in the final stages the intelligent aid of Betty G. Seaver was of great assistance. The interest and encouragement of Dr. Ray A. Billington helped more than he can know.

There is no way by which I can express to my wife, Frances Borglum Moore, what her deciphering of my first drafts, her research, and her understanding did to carry the book to completion. To her I have dedicated the book.

Edmund A. Moore

Storrs, Connecticut
May, 1956

Acknowledgments

The author wishes to thank the following for permission to quote copyright material: Dodd, Mead & Company, Inc., for a quotation from *Grover Cleveland, A Study in Courage*, by Allan Nevins, copyright 1932 by Allan Nevins; Duke University Press for quotations from *Bishop Cannon's Own Story*, edited by Richard L. Watson, Jr., copyright 1955 by Duke University Press; Harcourt, Brace & Company, Inc., for a quotation from *The Ku Klux Klan: A Study of the American Mind*, by John Moffatt Mecklin, copyright 1924 by Harcourt, Brace & Company, Inc.; Harper and Brothers for quotations from *As I Knew Them*, by Henry L. Stoddard, copyright 1927 by Harper and Brothers, and from *Church and State in the United States*, by Anson Phelps Stokes, copyright 1950 by Harper and Brothers; Henry Holt & Company for quotations from *William Allen White's America*, by Walter Johnson, copyright 1946 by Henry Holt & Company; Little, Brown & Company for quotations from *Atlantic Harvest*, by Ellery Sedgwick, copyright 1947 by Little, Brown & Company; The Macmillan Company for quotations from *Memoirs of Herbert Hoover*, by Herbert Hoover, copyright 1952 by The Macmillan Company, and from *The Story of American Catholicism*, by Theodore

Maynard, copyright 1951 by The Macmillan Company; Viking Press, Inc., for a quotation from *Up To Now*, by Alfred E. Smith, copyright 1929 by Viking Press, Inc.; and Brandt & Brandt for a quotation from *The Shadow of the Pope*, by Michael Williams, published by McGraw-Hill Book Company, Inc., copyright 1932 by Michael Williams.

The author is also grateful to the following newspapers and periodicals for permission to use material from their publications: *America*, *Atlantic*, *Catholic Telegraph*, *Christian Register*, *Collier's*, *Commonweal*, Houston *Chronicle*, Houston *Post-Dispatch*, New York *Herald Tribune*, *The New York Times*, New York *World* (Press Publishing Company), and Washington *Post and Times Herald*.

Contents

CHAPTER		PAGE
1	The Anti-Catholic Heritage, to World War I	1
2	"An Unwritten Law"	21
3	The Marshall-Smith Exchange	57
4	Enter Tom Heflin and Tom Walsh	81
5	A Campaign Within a Campaign	107
6	Anti-Catholicism at Flood Stage	145
	Conclusion	195
	References	201
	Bibliographical Note	209
	Index	213

Illustrations

PAGE

Alfred E. Smith as Governor of New York . . Frontispiece

"Rome Never Changes, Boast of Vatican" 25

"The Pope Sends Another Pole Expedition" 46

"A Heavy Load for Al" 84

"Cabinet Meeting—If Al Were President" 109

Alfred E. Smith with John J. Raskob 123

"Though I speak with the tongues of men and angels . . ." 139

"The Wet 'Hope' " 161

"The Al Smiths! Oh, My Dear!" 167

"The Pinch Hitter" 177

Governor Smith's Notes for his Oklahoma City Speech . 181

Alfred E. Smith and Franklin D. Roosevelt 197

A Catholic Runs for President

CHAPTER ONE

The Anti-Catholic Heritage, to World War I

> . . . Behold that Man of Sin, the Pope, worthy thy utmost Hatred.[1] —*The New-England Primer*

There can be no serious doubt what the central figure in the drama thought about his fate in the election of 1928. Alfred E. Smith, Governor of New York and Democratic candidate for the presidency, was convinced that he lost the election in large part because of the whispering campaign conducted against him and that his religion furnished much of the basis for that campaign.[2] The future biographer of the great Governor will be embarrassed, as the writer has been to a much less degree, by the failure of the central figure to soliloquize for the record; and he will be plagued by the fact that Smith customarily did his business orally in conference, leaving no record of it for the biographer. Smith's *Autobiography* is a pale replica indeed of its author and serves us little. Yet the problem here is less irksome since there is not a Prince of Denmark in our story but, rather, an issue or a crusade. Of course, the career and fate of Smith is a connecting link in all that follows.

There were many reasons why Alfred E. Smith did not become President of the United States. His attempt to win the nomination in 1924 failed. He was nominated in 1928, but that was a year in which Americans basked in the warmth of Republican prosperity. Many of the country's industrial leaders in the twenties agreed with Henry Ford that one of the great props of the edifice of material satisfaction was the Prohibition Amendment. Each party was split within itself on the question of the efficacy and wisdom of that Amendment. On the maintenance of the prosperity issue the Republicans, who had long enjoyed the special confidence of businessmen, had an immense advantage. While boom times continued, it was hard to imagine the return of the Democrats to power. A new and complicated issue was added when the Democrats nominated for the presidency a man clearly identified as the leading spokesman and symbol of a newer, urban America. Quite appropriately this leader was a Roman Catholic, the first to be so nominated by a major party.

Anyone not conversant with the American past might well ask why the running of a Catholic for president should be considered remarkable. History supplies the answer. For a century and a half the English colonies in America had Catholic neighbors on the north, west, and south. In this situation Catholicism suggested a particularly militant kind of political Romanism. The Revolutionary War reduced, at least for the time, the intensity of this feeling, for His Catholic Majesty of Spain and His Christian Majesty of France were both more or less allied with the United States against Great Britain. For two generations after the Revolution anti-Catholicism was less violent than either before or after. Fear of political Catholicism could not greatly flourish in the age of Bishop John Carroll, the leading American Catholic of the Revolutionary era and a member of a great and respected family. With the exception of the faithful in Louisiana, Catholics of the first few decades of the national period were usually English in background and well assimilated. An effort was made by the Catholic laity in the early decades of the nineteenth century to place the control of Church properties in their own hands. The movement, known as trusteeism, illustrates the tendency of institutions and practices in the United States to adjust to the democratic environment. Its failure strengthened the popular conviction that Catholicism could not so adapt itself in the United States. Memories of this aberration from Catholic theory and practice may well have been alive at the Vatican more than half a century later when there were insistent rumors that Catholics in the United States were deviating from universal Catholicism.[3]

The second quarter of the last century brought profound changes in the status of Catholicism vis-à-vis American society. Famine and other maladjustments in Europe sent great numbers of Catholics, and especially Irish Catholics, to the United States. The majority of these immigrants were abjectly poor. They were regarded as the docile followers of their priests in politics, as natural slum-dwellers, and as Catholics who had neither the standing in the community nor the culture of their coreligionists in the years before the great Irish migrations. Many Protestants insisted that the country was in danger of speedily becoming Catholic. This conviction helps explain why the decades before the Civil War were marred by political nativism. By the eighteen thirties the antiforeign spirit had produced a reinvigorated anti-Catholicism that diminished little until dispelled by the clouds of Civil War. After an orgy of the burning of Catholic properties came the high point in political anti-Catholicism, the Know-Nothing party of the eighteen fifties.* For a brief interlude nativism, with anti-Catholicism a basic ingredient, challenged the primacy of the slavery issue. When sectional hostility erupted into war, charges were made that the Civil War itself was brought on by the secret machinations of the Jesuits.

Certain official pronouncements of the Church during and soon after the Civil War revived the fears of intelligent non-Catholics. The *Syllabus of Errors*, promulgated by Pius IX in 1864, convinced many that the Catholic church was in league with the forces of

* This phase of the history of anti-Catholicism has been told authoritatively by Ray Allen Billington in *The Protestant Crusade, 1800-1860* (New York, 1938). Billington's book is basic for an understanding of the problem up to the Civil War. For post-Civil War anti-Catholicism there is no strictly comparable study, although John Higham's *Strangers in the Land* (New Brunswick, N. J., 1955) briefly approximates it in a more comprehensive undertaking.

reaction. This document censured as "errors" much of the liberal thought of the nineteenth century. It was interpreted as a rejection of the idea of tolerance—this to the discomfiture of many Catholics who accepted democracy and religious liberty. Hard on the *Syllabus* came the Proclamation of the Dogma of Papal Infallibility by the Vatican Council of 1869–1870. This dogma appeared to many to demonstrate decisively the antithetical positions of American democracy and Roman absolutism. That the pontiff's words were infallible only when he spoke, *ex cathedra*, on matters of faith and morals helped little to dispel the bad impression made by the Encyclical in the United States. Newspapers throughout the country deplored the Council's Act.[4] Under Leo XIII (1878–1903) tension was somewhat relaxed, but the new Pope did not retreat from the general position his predecessor had taken in condemning much that was characteristic of modern liberalism and nationalism.

Leo's reign was marked by a number of controversies within the Catholic church in the United States. Most important were the struggles over Cahenslyism and the contest over Americanism, each worthy of attention in a background sketch. In the United States the name of Peter Cahensly suggested the effort to retain national divisions among Catholics in America. German Catholics led by Cahensly were concerned because American Catholics of German extraction were in some instances served by non-German, usually Irish, priests and bishops. Followers of Cahensly urged that each group be placed under spiritual shepherds of its own nationality.

Indeed, this demand had been a powerful one in the early part of the nineteenth century. Victory for the Cahenslyans was theoretically impossible within Catholic tradition, and in fact they did not triumph, to the good of both church and state. At a later time James Cardinal Gibbons expressed himself as "firmly convinced that nationalist groups in the Church would tend to become political elements."[5] The movement itself increased the suspicion of the non-Catholic community which needed little additional evidence on which to build the argument that the Catholic church in the United States was a divisive and therefore a dangerous institution.

If the Cahensly movement, though defeated, raised doubts in some minds about the capacity of the Catholic church to advance the process of Americanization, the perplexing controversy in the Church known as Americanism had a sad denouement that again raised fears about Catholicism. The reader may be confused by the uses to which the root word "American" has been put. Americanization is a reasonably clear word, but the controversy within the Church known as Americanism is far from self-explanatory. The temptation to "define" it obliquely seems almost irresistible and may, indeed, be the most prudent course since the controversy was about a "phantom heresy." If the reader turns to *The Catholic Encyclopedia*, under "Americanism," he is referred to the heading *Testem Benevolentiae*. There he will find no precise definition of Americanism; he is, however, made aware that the controversy was no isolated one in the history of the Church in the nineteenth century and that it revolved about a foreboding lest new methods and new beliefs amounting to heresy might have permeated parts of the Church in the United States. The resulting concern touched directly on the preservation of old and established truths. There was apprehension about short-cuts, including even the possible dilution of dogma with the aim of increasing the rate of conversions. The term "Americanism" also suggests the concern that there might be at work a tendency toward a national church in the United States.

The nuances of the controversy were important, and so, too, were the confusion and misunderstanding that pervaded the issue as it was discussed abroad. An impression had been created in some European Catholic circles, in the late nineteenth century, that there was indeed a dangerous deviation within the American Church in the direction of a quasi-heretical accommodation with nationalism and nineteenth-century liberal ideas. Leo XIII himself was sufficiently concerned finally to condemn as errors the allegations most frequently made against the supposed views of the so-called liberal American bishops. Foremost among these were Baltimore's Cardinal James Gibbons and St. Paul's Archbishop John Ireland. Each of these high dignitaries of the Catholic church had often praised American democratic institutions including the American practice of separating church and state. Each was of course sure that, in so doing, his loyalty to the universal Church was in no way weakened. Each was regarded by Presidents and other eminent Americans as an exemplar and exponent of American principles as well as a loyal servant of his Church. Each attempted, with considerable success, to interpret his Church to non-Catholic Americans; each was a friend of the American public school, though devoted to the schools of his Church.

It would, therefore, not be a matter of indifference if the highest authority in the Roman Catholic church were even to seem to condemn the views of the liberal wing of the hierarchy. The controversy was exceedingly complicated and many-sided. On January 22, 1899, the Pope brought sorrow, though prompt acceptance, to the hearts of Gibbons and those American bishops who had hoped that Leo would take no formal notice of the complaints of the conservatives. The Pope's action was in the form of an Apostolic Letter, *Testem Benevolentiae*, to Cardinal Gibbons. The Letter was not a direct condemnation but was interpreted as a defeat for the liberal wing of the hierarchy, and, by some non-Catholics, as proof that the Church could never adapt itself to American ways.* Says *The Catholic Encyclopedia*, quoting in part from *Testem Benevolentiae:*

> The Letter concludes with a brief exhortation for unity, as against a spirit that would tend towards developing a national Church. The term Americanism is approved as applying to the characteristic qualities which reflect honour on the American people, . . . "If by that name be designated the characteristic qualities which reflect honour on the people of America, just as other nations have what is special to them; or, if it implies the condition of your commonwealths, or the laws and customs prevailing in them, there is no reason why we should deem that it ought to be discarded. But if it is to be used not only to sig-

* See Note on Americanism, pp. 18–19.

nify, but even to commend the above doctrines, there can be no doubt that our venerable brethren, the bishops of America, would be the first to repudiate and condemn it, as being especially unjust to them and to the entire nation as well. For it raises the suspicion that there are some among you who conceive and desire a Church in America different from that which is in the rest of the world."[6]

One reason why Rome's "condemnation" of Americanism brought sorrow to the Gibbons-Ireland wing of the American hierarchy is that there was a reasonable fear that it would add fuel to the fires of anti-Catholicism. No recent generation has been without the activities of some organization that lived by castigating Catholics. In the eighteen nineties and to a decreasing extent in the first years of the present century the "No-Popery" feeling was fairly well organized. Most important of the anti-Romanist organizations was the American Protective Association, commonly known as the A.P.A.[7] Never as strong as the Know-Nothing movement of the eighteen fifties and never a political party, the A.P.A. was the most important anti-Catholic organization to arise between the mid-nineteenth century and the period of revived anti-Catholicism in the nineteen twenties. Its influence was considerable in several of the northern and, especially, western states. In national politics its weight was most felt in 1896, when it attempted to defeat McKinley. For several years it was something of a thorn in the side of the Republican party. In the long history of organized anti-Catholicism the A.P.A. showed few unique features, but it is noteworthy that its decline, very soon after the turn of the century, came at a time when the sons and grandsons of Irish Catholic immigrants had risen far above the humble origins of their forebears. By World War I the rise of Catholics to a higher economic level had produced a new attitude on the part of Catholics toward attacks on their religion.

Testem Benevolentiae caused sorrow and concern; it did not, however, condemn Gibbons and those who looked to him for spiritual leadership, for revering and applauding their country's institutions. This Gibbons never ceased to do. Ten years after Leo's Letter the Cardinal, without departing from the purest Catholic doctrine, assured his countrymen that the Catholics in America

> . . . prefer its American form of government before any other. . . . They accept the Constitution without reserve, with no desire, as Catholics, to see it changed in any feature. They can with a clear conscience swear to uphold it. . . . But while the union [of church and state] is ideally best, history assuredly does not prove that it is always practically best. There is a union that is inimical to the interests of religion, and consequently to the State. . . . there is a separation that is for the best interests of both. In our country separation is a necessity; and it is a separation that works best for the interests of religion, as Mr. Taft recently stated, as well as for the good of the State.[8]

This was a frank statement which met with no dissent in Rome and which satisfied many, though far from all, Americans.

Almost two decades later, in 1927, substantially the same issue was revived in a challenge to the leading contender for the Democratic nomination for President, Alfred E. Smith. Thoughtful Americans, Protestants and Catholics, then went back to Gibbons' classic statements. Americanism in its usual meaning, rather than in the special sense of the controversy ended by Leo's Letter to Gibbons, continued to be expressed and demonstrated by most Catholics as well as non-Catholics, both by word and deed. During the presidencies of Theodore Roosevelt, Taft, and Wilson no Catholic and no American symbolized true patriotism to a higher degree than Gibbons. The Baltimore Cardinal was respected and loved by Americans of differing faiths. Long after his death, in 1921, his life and praise of American institutions became a refutation of the calumnies of bigots. The anti-Catholic battalions were not, however, dissolved by the calm spirit and stalwart Americanism of the Baltimore Cardinal nor by the daily conduct of American Catholics.

Some reminders of the frenetic activities of those who saw popish plots on the eve of and during World War I will make it plain that the anti-Romanists of the nineteen twenties did not have to go far back for historical succor. An incident in the political history of the eighteen eighties, when the Republicans had long had control of the executive branch of the government, furnished ammunition for future use. Out of it came one of those slogans that attains almost the weight of a new historical cause. Its common use justifies a slight digression. The incident was a by-product of the presidential campaign of 1884. With the popular Blaine, "the man from Maine," as the Republican candidate, prospects that the Democrats would break the twenty-odd-year hold of the G.O.P. on the White House were less than rosy. If Blaine had failed to present himself before the voters as impeccably honest in the conduct of public business, he had the offsetting advantage that Victorian ethics assigned first place to private morality. On this score the Democratic candidate, Grover Cleveland, a man of sterling honesty, had a blemish on his early personal record. Though his later conduct was marked by honor and candor, no one could be sure that Christian charity and common sense would offset the political damage to Cleveland's prospects.

A devastating slogan almost certainly turned the election in favor of Cleveland. The pertinent facts are few. At New York's Fifth Avenue Hotel, on October 29, a "crowd of obscure clergymen" met a badly fatigued Blaine. At that meeting a Presbyterian minister, the Reverend Samuel D. Burchard, referred to the Democratic party as the party of "Rum, Romanism and Rebellion." Neither Blaine nor the attending newspapermen caught the remark, but a shadowing shorthand reporter in the employ of the Democrats brought the verbal dynamite to party headquarters, a block away. Within hours the large cities of the United States were "placarded with the insulting alliteration."[9] Henry L. Stoddard, one of the newspapermen who missed the remark, reports that by "late afternoon the city was flooded with sensational circulars intended to arouse Catholic voters."[10] Blaine's repudiation of the Burchard remark was tardy; the damage was done. The phrase was equivalent to a charge that the Democratic party was composed of saloon keepers, the kind of priests depicted in anti-Catholic cartoons, "rum soaked" politicians of Irish extraction, and the spiritual allies of

Jefferson Davis. The Republicans had counted on Blaine, whose relatives included Catholics, to attract some Democratic voters. There is no reason to doubt that the Burchard slogan backfired in New York State to at least the extent of eleven hundred votes, the margin of Cleveland's victory in the Empire State.* That was enough to elect him. No wonder "Rum, Romanism and Rebellion" carried authority in later years, including 1928. That it became the valued property of the bigots attacking Catholics is one of the lesser ironies of history.

The early years of the present century saw the decline and final passing of the American Protective Association. Its political power had never equaled that of the Know-Nothings half a century earlier. Other and weaker anti-Catholic organizations partly filled the void, and occasionally the issue played a part, though never a decisive one, in national politics. In the Taft-Bryan campaign of 1908, the Republican candidate was accused of pro- and anti-Catholicism, the while he was denounced as a Unitarian. The attack on Taft as pro-Catholic harked back to his success in settling the Friars' land dispute after the Spanish-American War. The Vatican was, of course, a party to the negotiations, and that is all that was needed to raise the cry of favoritism toward Catholic interests. Not long before this, Theodore Roosevelt had felt the sting of the "No-Popery" brigade. He was charged with exerting pressure on the

* The contemporary estimate was that the clever use of the slogan by the Democrats cost Blaine four or five times the margin of votes by which he lost New York State and the election.

Vatican to bestow the red hat on Archbishop Ireland. Roosevelt greatly admired Ireland's brand of Americanism, but for his trouble and lack of carefulness he was accused of trying to garner Catholic votes for the Republican party.[11]

Despite occasional flurries of this kind, as World War I approached there was some promise of a new and better day in Catholic-Protestant relations. The anti-Catholicism of 1910 was much less pregnant with danger for the country than was the brand of the eighteen fifties. An example of better Protestant-Catholic relations was reflected in a 1911 testimonial meeting for Cardinal Gibbons. It was the occasion of the fiftieth anniversary of his priesthood and the twenty-fifth of his cardinalate. Eighteen thousand people stood three hours to hear President Taft, former President Roosevelt, and other leaders do honor to the man and to the spirit he exemplified. It was on this occasion that Roosevelt declared that the future would see "Presidents who are Catholics as well as Presidents who are Protestants; if we live long enough, Presidents who are Jews as well as Presidents who are Gentiles."[12] The forecast drew great applause.

Roosevelt's prophecy was not soon to be realized, but efforts to attain real rather than superficial understanding were increasing on the eve of World War I. On rare occasions the hope of reconciliation was expressed in its deepest religious and philosophical meaning. Declarations were made that Catholics and Protestants ought to recognize that their common enemy was materialism and irreligion. Catholic Bishop McFaul of

Trenton wrote that it behooves Protestants and Catholics to ". . . forget their petty jealousies and indifferences and, altho holding fast to their religious convictions, to unite, to stand shoulder to shoulder, forming an impregnable barrier to antichristian doctrine and pagan morals."[13]

Professional Catholic baiters, as though to combat appeals for broader cooperation, increased their efforts. Most important and notorious of their papers was the *Menace*, published at Aurora, Missouri. Claiming a circulation of over a million in 1912, *Menace* was rankly anti-Catholic. Its every issue was sensational. Its officers, if not legally, were morally guilty of publishing and using the mails to disseminate "obscene, lewd, lascivious, filthy and indecent matter . . ." to quote from an indictment against the officers of the *Menace*.[14] President Taft and the postal authorities were blamed for allowing it the use of the mails.*

Filling, though not fully, the void left by the decline of the American Protective Association were new organizations such as the Covenanters, the Guardians of Liberty, and the Knights of Luther. All of them by 1914 were engaged in battling the pope. The Covenanters pledged themselves to oppose Catholic candidates

* In 1914 Gibbons opposed the suppression of the *Menace*. He felt that, regardless of the abuse it heaped on his Church and him, barring it from the mails would only strengthen other anti-Catholic publications and would do violence to the American ideal of freedom of the press. Then, as in the twenties, the mails usually remained available to anti-Catholic literature. The whole subject of the use and abuse of the mails, as well as the legal aspects of extreme anti-Catholicism, is a complicated one.[15]

for public office and even to refrain from business relations with Catholics. The Guardians of Liberty, emphasizing restriction of immigration, had turned openly to anti-Catholicism in 1912, the change brought about by the efforts of the rabidly anti-Catholic Tom Watson of Georgia. Organizations established for other purposes attempted to widen their appeal by capitalizing on the fear of Rome. In Florida, for example, the Prohibitionists pledged that "No one shall be qualified to hold office who owes allegiance to any foreign sovereign, potentate or ecclesiastic, or who admits the right, either human or divine, of such a one to control his actions."[16]

If the "No-Popery" crusaders occasionally embarrassed Roosevelt and Taft, a more irritating barrage was laid down against Wilson. His first administration marked the apex of an era of progressivism which was not confined to politics alone. But signs pointed in opposite directions in the area of religious tolerance. There was a growing feeling that the relations between two great divisions of Christianity were in keeping neither with the spirit of the age nor with Christ's teaching.[17] Despite this, the years immediately preceding the entrance of the United States into the War to Save Democracy were marred by certain events that nourished anti-Catholic feeling and agitation. The supply of the old venom was not exhausted, and the specific irritants in the Wilson period were sufficient to divert some of the bigotry into the main stream of public life.

The formulation of United States policy toward the social revolution in Mexico was perhaps bound to excite old fears. Catholics complained that the recognition of the Carranza government was an act injurious to their religion. From some in the opposite camp came charges that the President was pro-Catholic. Wilson's private secretary, Joseph P. Tumulty, was a Catholic and a New Jersey progressive; bigots called him a spy in the White House. He was charged with failing to call Wilson's attention to each new and wild warning that the Pope, through Tumulty, was about to take control of the government in Washington. Aggressive anti-Catholics called for Tumulty's scalp. When Wilson ignored the noise, he was denounced for violating the right of petition. Tumulty had acted, of course, in a manner appropriate to the duties of a private secretary, whether Catholic, Protestant, or agnostic.

The response of Catholic leaders to the new signs of bigotry was markedly different in 1914–1915 from the basically cautious attitude exhibited at the turn of the century. Then the A.P.A. was believed capable of using to its own advantage any aggressive defense Catholic leaders might offer. Now, on the eve of World War I, Catholics were more prosperous, more influential in secular society, and more disinclined to accept a cautious course simply because protest conceivably could aid bigots. Catholic leaders were inclined to favor a bolder policy as one that would better serve the interests of both church and state. In this spirit the Knights of Columbus established, in 1915, a Commission on Religious Prejudices. The aim was to analyze the malady of intolerance and to make recommendations. The leading spirit on the Commission was a Louisville businessman, Colonel P. H. Callahan. The Commission's report condemned the Guardians of Liberty and all other instruments of bigotry. On the whole, the tone of the report was optimistic. There was hope that a better day was dawning despite the murky corners where light had not yet penetrated.

Note on Americanism

The controversy over Americanism is complicated. Its human side is well portrayed by Ellis, *Gibbons*, Vol. II, pp. 1-80, and by another Catholic scholar, Maynard, *American Catholicism*, pp. 498-521. There is brief coverage in the monumental volumes by the Episcopal historian Anson Phelps Stokes, *Church and State in the United States*, Vol. II, pp. 356-60. Much of the controversy, as carried on in Europe without complete understanding of special American conditions, revolved about the alleged teaching of Father Isaac Hecker, a leader in the highly influential Paulist order. A faulty understanding of what he had advocated made Hecker a controversial figure, especially among French Catholics. The charge, in Maynard's words, was that

> . . . Hecker was advocating an accommodation of Catholic dogma to the temper of the American Protestant public. But what Hecker really said was: "So far as is compatible with faith and piety, I am for accepting the American civilization with its usages and customs; leaving aside other reasons, it is the only way by which Catholicism can become the religion of our people." . . . This is not a Procrustean fitting of Catholicism to America but a perception that American institutions are of their very nature favorable to Catholicism. (p. 515)

This however does not satisfy Maynard, who writes also of *Testem Benevolentiae*:

> But despite all this—or because of it—Rome had some reason to be alarmed when books and articles began to appear in France and Italy (especially France) setting out notions said to have been derived from some of the most eminent American ecclesiastics. . . . the captains of the Church in the United States had spoken so strongly . . . about the desirability of the separation of Church and

State as a practical advantage—that not without reason were many Roman officials uneasy. It was to stop the process before it went any further that the Pope spoke out; and never were any people so dumbfounded with astonishment or, one might add, so hurt, as those who understood that the *Testem Benevolentiae* was aimed at themselves. (p. 501)

On balance, Maynard thinks that *Testem Benevolentiae* was needed preventive medicine:

In the main it was the making sure that such erroneous opinions would never arise in this country. The shock, though humiliating to Americans, was salutary: they were put on their guard. It might easily have happened that "streamlined" apologetics would have come into being and in time have verged towards the errors the Pope listed. All likelihood of that was now over. The heresy was destroyed before it had taken shape. Rome had caught something in the air—a readiness to yield to the *Zeitgeist* to win souls by accommodation. It was no more than a vague incipience. But it would quite possibly have developed and hardened had not Leo spoken. (p. 517)

CHAPTER TWO

"An Unwritten Law"

"No Governor can kiss the papal ring and get within gunshot of the White House. . ."[1]
—Bishop Adna W. Leonard

The year 1918, when President Wilson suffered his first political defeat, marked Smith's first election as Governor of New York. It was clear that the War for Democracy had not ushered in the millenium; the Era of Progressivism, however, did not everywhere end so abruptly as the apostles of normalcy had hoped. The task of adjusting legal codes to serve the ends of social justice in an industrial society, still mainly one for the states, remained urgent. At the moment when frustration and futility were triumphant in Washington, Governor Smith carried through humanitarian and administrative reforms in the Empire State and held ascendancy over both political parties. A master of practical political science without benefit of academic degrees, he had the uncommon ability to make "the record" plain to ordinary people. He was to be five times a candidate for governor and in his only defeat, in 1920, gained prestige by running remarkably well despite the great swing of a tired people away from Wilsonian idealism. Smith's name had been offered the same year in nomination at his party's national convention at San Francisco, but more as a gesture than with serious intent. The first concerted efforts to make him President were directed toward 1924. His election in 1922 to a second term as Governor automatically insured his serious consideration for the presidential nomination in 1924. There were other strong contenders for the nomination, but Smith's second election by a record-breaking majority inevitably evoked memories of Tilden, Cleveland, and other great New York Democrats who had become their party's nominees for President. So far, no Catholic had won a major party nomination, but there had been no communicant of the Roman church with anything approaching Smith's combination of personal and political claims. Would the Governor's religion be a factor in denying his party's highest gift to one otherwise so available? There were objections to Smith other than his religion. One was his strong opposition to statutory Prohibition. Although a growing number of Americans questioned the religious, economic, and constitutional presuppositions that underlay the Eighteenth Amendment and the Volstead Act, these voters appear to have been a minority even in the late nineteen twenties. Al Smith's wetness, highlighted by his much-discussed support for the repeal of his own state's legislation to enforce the Volstead Act, was scarcely a political asset outside the Northeast.

The revelation that Smith was a Catholic—a New York City, Irish Catholic—was impressed upon the country's consciousness in the months after his thumping 1922 victory had frightened the professional anti-Catholics, especially the leaders of the Ku Klux Klan. Though members of this and similar organizations openly attacked him on religious grounds—almost always making simultaneous protest that they were doing no such thing—religion was properly dubbed the "silent issue"; it was neither polite nor politically astute to discuss it, at least audibly. Smart politicians often denied its existence. However, Catholic diocesan papers ran serialized historical articles which surveyed the story of anti-Catholicism in American history. Was it conceivable that the twenties of the Century of Progress might offer fertile soil for a recurrence on a broad national scale of political anti-Catholicism? There was a widespread disposition among liberal non-Catholics to assign such activities to the past, to assume in a spirit of easy tolerance that the influence within Catholicism of such leaders as Archbishop Ireland and Cardinal Gibbons had so Americanized the ancient Church as to close forever a long and unworthy chapter in American history. Yet the postwar era was marked by cynicism and boredom. In middle-class America there was an increasing disposition to question all supposed departures from old American norms, and there were in the land many self-appointed defenders of America—of a white, native, Fundamentalist Protestant America.

The twentieth-century Klan came into being in

1915. Its growth up to 1920 was slow, but the next three or four years were very lush ones for Klan organizers. The new organization had some of the objectives of its namesake of post-Civil War days. Like the old Klan it appealed to those with a love for mystery and secrecy, to many whose lives were drab, and to those who had need of a scapegoat. White supremacy was second to none on the list of Klan objectives. When many Americans were persuaded that this principle was in some manner threatened by aliens, Jews, and Catholics, the sum of hatred exceeded the parts. The Klan flourished in Long Island, New York, and in Oregon as well as throughout much of the Middle West and South. Reasons other than a vigilante insistence on white supremacy accounted for its success. Fear of Bolshevism, opposition to all things foreign, anti-Semitism, and anti-Catholicism were its other principal points of appeal, and they help explain its multisectional strength. To many the Klan seemed to be an effective means of preserving order and of helping to perpetuate the Protestant, Anglo-Saxon tradition in the United States. The Klan was strongly Fundamentalist, though affiliated with no denomination. Indeed, and in a broader view, it could not have succeeded had its program been hostile to the things held sacred by great numbers of Americans. A contemporary student of the Klan held:

> The Klan is not alien to American society. . . . The Klan is but the recrudescence of forces that already existed in American society, some of them recent, others dating from the more distant past. . . . [it] . . . draws its inspirations from ancient prejudices, classical hatreds, and ingrained social habits.[2]

Rome Never Changes, Boast of Vatican

This Klan cartoon from The Fellowship Forum *expresses the widespread concern over the church-state issue and the conviction that Catholicism might destroy the public school system.*

The strongholds of the Ku Klux Klan were the small towns and villages, where the older American stock dominated. The great majority of citizens in these communities were Protestants who knew very little of Catholics or of the immigrant stock of distant cities, but this in no way lessened their sense of apprehensiveness. In the rich Klan territory of the Middle West no single reason for the organization's success outweighed the exploitation of hostility toward the Roman Catholic church. In the South especially, anti-Semitism and anti-Catholicism were usually linked in Klan propaganda. Tammany Hall was denounced as the machine through which undesirable aliens planned first to seize control of the Democratic party, then of the government in Washington. Often the Klan attacked on more than one front. The flames of religious bigotry were fed by charges that the Catholic church had organized southern Negroes without regard to regional mores.[3] The Klan ransacked the entire past of anti-Catholicism for its list of accusations. Americans were asked to believe that the Knights of Columbus was an organization pledged to exterminate Protestants, that Catholic churches were arsenals, and that Catholics were responsible for the assassination of all Presidents who had met that fate. To advance its ends the Klan used propaganda literature, political pressure, and lawlessness. Of very great importance was the fact that many Americans did not join the Klan but were sympathetic with at least some of its aims. This was the organization that boasted, in 1923, that in the following year it would control both the Democratic and Republican conventions. It was more than idle boasting, for many politicians were afraid to oppose the Hooded Order; re-election for many might well depend on neutrality if not outright espousal of the Klan's ends. It was an ominous boast, and it was pointed above all to one special objective, undertaken in the name of all of the Klan's principal aims, racial, social, and religious. That objective was the destruction of the presidential ambitions of the brilliant politician-statesman, the Governor of New York, Alfred E. Smith.

Such was the stage on which Al Smith made his nationwide political debut in 1924. Since New York City was felt by many rural and small-town Americans to be the least American part of America, the selection of that city for the Democratic national convention, itself a victory for the Smith forces, increased the chances of an explosion in the party. Klan propaganda bristled with defiance. For the first time a Catholic of great prominence was about to make a serious bid for a major party nomination. Current periodicals discussed this novel situation and pointed out that never before had so able, popular, and otherwise available a Catholic reached such exalted political heights. Already there were portents that if Smith were to be defeated by a representative of the rural, dry, and Protestant areas, many would attribute it mainly to religious prejudice.

There was sufficient apprehension about the political liability inherent in Smith's religion to move some of his more ardent friends to try to meet this objection before the delegates assembled at Madison Square Garden. Since any defense involved some discussion of the delicate religious issue and therefore threatened to open further the floodgates of bigotry, it is not strange that some of Smith's more enthusiastic backers sometimes displayed a defiant spirit. A former Washington official, Frank P. Walsh, told a party gathering that Al Smith "would dissipate the belief held by many that 'a man of a certain religious faith' could not become President of the United States."[4] Smith, he said, would "wipe out that unwritten law."* A day later *The New York Times* reported a similar but more sweeping statement made before a gathering of policemen by a New York county judge, J. Harry Tiernan. Stung by the Republican claim that a Catholic could not hope for the presidency, the judge was cheered as he said that Catholics would resent any failure of Governor Smith to win the Democratic nomination for President for ignoble reasons. Catholics would "defy the American people to defeat him solely because of his religion."[5]

On the eve of the 1924 Democratic national convention a Catholic priest, Paul L. Blakely, S.J., speculated on the strength of the religious obstacle. He noted a reduction in religious prejudice but confessed to some puzzlement caused by the unresolved problem he saw

* The notion that there is some kind of a Constitutional exclusion of Catholics from the presidency is one which the writer encountered frequently, especially in private papers. A typical example of it in print is the pamphlet "America's Two Unwritten Laws," by E. A. (only the initials of the author were given) in the writer's possession. It appears that some thought the denial of the presidency to Catholics was in the text of the Constitution, while others, a bit more sophisticated, were sure that it must be considered a part of our unwritten Constitution. The second of the "unwritten laws" was the denial to any president of a third term. The pamphlet antedated by a dozen years F. D. R.'s election to a third term.

as the attitude of mind that was typified by politics at Cranberry Corners: "Said the chairman of the Cracker-Barrel Congress at Cranberry Corners: 'Ain't there a law agin' Cath'lics bein' President? If there ain't, there orter be.' "[6] The events of the next four years were to justify amply Father Blakely's concern.

Although the general-circulation periodicals gave relatively little space to Catholicism as a political issue until 1926 and 1927, the *Forum* discussed the delicate subject under the title "Can a Catholic be President?" a few days before the 1924 convention opened.[7] The author of the article, Martin Conboy, was a prominent Catholic of New York City. He painted a favorable statistical picture, then reasoned "intuitively" to reach an affirmative answer to the question. He arrived at his conclusion by a strange combination of evidence. First, he stressed the leading position of the Catholic church among the churches in many states, but then he continued with the apparent *non sequitur* that "there is not and never has been any such thing as a Catholic vote."[8] He then offered a balance sheet by denominations. Episcopalians, Quakers, Congregationalists, and Unitarians were credited with having little if any religious intolerance. Conboy felt "reasonably sure" about the Episcopalians and Quakers and "intuitively so" about the Congregationalists and Unitarians. He was sure that the Jews of the great urban areas would not discriminate against a Catholic; some Presbyterians would be undependable and "Southern and middle States" Methodists and Baptists could be expected to behave very badly.[9]

The use of the word "religious" as appropriate to the

kind of opposition that existed toward a candidate who was a Catholic, a wet, and a product of an urban, East Side New York environment raises the question whether the part has not been taken for the whole. The need to see the problem in its sociological entirety may sometimes be evidenced in small but revealing matters. A seemingly trivial example appeared in a small literary excursion into the subject of family names. On the eve of the Madison Square convention Homer Joseph Dodge asked in the *Forum:*

> What sterling, hundred-per-cent-plus, Nordic American can frown upon one bearing such names as Al and Smith, ask his friends? . . . Is it possible the American people will permit one born in a log cabin to reach the White House while they close the part to a barefoot fish-child?
>
> . . .
>
> Al Smith probably is the first Roman Catholic who many people have seriously believed could be elected President. They recognize that he would have the opposition of the type of crusading Protestant who believes that Rome reigns secretly all over the world. . . . Nevertheless, they believe enough other Americans live who can be convinced that a fundamental difference exists between Catholics of the name of Smith and Catholics of the name of Murphy.[10]

One is tempted to conclude that the Democratic party was predestined to suffer defeat in all three presidential elections in the twenties. Perhaps there is a degree of hindsight in this view, however, for early in 1924 there seemed to be a substantial opportunity for victory. Revelations of Republican scandals were fresh, and Josephus Daniels suggested that the platform establish a record for brevity and consist solely of the Commandment "Thou shalt not steal." But streamlined political crusading was ruled out. Public apathy and the divisive La Follette third-party candidacy help explain why Republican good fortune continued through 1924. The elevation of Calvin Coolidge to the presidency reassured Republicans who were disturbed by the evidence of widespread corruption in the Harding administration. Yet the decisive contribution to Republican victory was the Donkey's own free gift offered up at the Garden. The paralyzing character and length of that Donnybrook Fair demonstrated a hopeless party division on the most sensitive issues and spoiled whatever opportunity there might have been for success in November. Republicans, lacking a southern wing, managed to avoid a head-on collision over the Klan issue. Democrats, however, with clashing southern and northeastern elements, permitted a long fight for a specific denunciation of the Hooded Order to set the stage for an interminable nomination contest. The nation's first radio audience for a convention was treated to a futile, 103-ballot performance. This, to all intents, destroyed any conceivable chance for Democratic victory.

The rural forces at Madison Square Garden were led by William Gibbs McAdoo, Wilson's son-in-law and member of his War cabinet. McAdoo had the misfortune, as legal counsel for oil interests, to have run afoul of public opinion. Though his prestige as a progressive was damaged, McAdoo was unwilling to withdraw from the race. But for the two-thirds rule he had the votes to win. Governor Smith, the challenger, could not have been ignored even had his achievement at Albany been less outstanding; with his impressive record he was bound to become a powerful contender. Triumphing over early subservience to Tammany—a feat denied by millions of Americans who used "Tammany" as a kind of fearsome expletive—Smith attracted the support of many independents and of some progressives of both parties.

The prospects for harmony at the Democratic convention of 1924 were negligible. The two wings of the party were so far apart on the most fundamental issues that even a leader as fortunately placed as Woodrow Wilson in 1912 would have had an almost superhuman task to weld the Democratic party into a fighting force. The scandals of the Harding administration seemed to spell opportunity. But neither Smith nor McAdoo—the latter now seemingly equated with the organization that practiced terror to preserve a static order—could unite the Democracy in time to defeat Calvin Coolidge, the symbol of Vermont virtue in the midst of Babylon. Though many Democratic leaders were pessimistic about party prospects before the first pounding of the gavel at Madison Square Garden, few foresaw a suicidal urge so serious that it would require a major depression to revive the patient. The delegates were too exhausted in body and purse to reach the 255th ballot humorously suggested by Franklin D. Roosevelt to Josephus Daniels as the likely end. Commenting in May on the prospect of a long convention, Roosevelt, who was one of Smith's right-hand supporters, wrote to Daniels, a McAdoo man, that the party might have to resort to the strategem of ". . . putting your present candidate and mine into a room together armed with a complete Navy outfit ranging from bean soup to 16″ guns with orders that only one man come out alive."*

As the balloting droned on at the great fight pavilion, it became increasingly clear that neither Smith nor McAdoo could win. McAdoo had the votes to stop Smith, but under the rules of the party the New Yorker had enough determined backers to block McAdoo. And so, on the 103d ballot delegates gave John W. Davis the empty honor of the nomination and of campaigning without any hope for success. The Republican strategy was to ignore Davis and concentrate on the ominous possibility that La Follette, regarded as a dangerous radical, might throw the election into the House of Representatives. For the Democrats the Davis nomination served as a stop-gap device, but the irreconcilable cleavages in the party had wrecked prospects for victory in November.

The division in the party on socio-cultural lines was everywhere apparent at the convention. The urban element had little understanding of or patience with the rural outlook. The sometimes raucous support which Smith received from his backers massed in the galleries confirmed the opinion of his opponents that common courtesy was not to be found in the motley population of Gotham. Suspicion and dislike of the metropolis was common among those who represented the hinterland. *The New York Times* recorded an amusing illustration of this in an editorial entitled "Wicked Hospitality." The occasion was what the *Times* called one

* Roosevelt's playful letter suggests that its author might be on the little end of a Daniels–Roosevelt ticket in 1928 or 1932.[11]

of McAdoo's "Sunday political hortations and dehortations," conducted for the edification of his delegates. According to the *Times*, McAdoo

> . . . warned his delegates and supporters against the perilous and treacherous hospitality of this town. The attentions and invitations and seeming kindnesses offered are but "devices put forth to assist the evil hosts to victory." . . . He wanted the faithful to stay in the hall and not to be lured away by the perfidious proffers of a hospitality "designed to put over a particular candidate." It has been noticed before that, as a candidate—and as a lawyer—Mr. McAdoo is not too particular. It might be thought that his homily was far from complimentary to the convention; but since New York is plunged in darkness and sin, it was his austere duty to chastise her, and his severe moral earnestness stirred a pious rapture in his congregation. "Don't let us eat another one of their [the New Yorkers'] olives or their chocolate eclaires," cried a woman delegate. We should say not. They might be poisoned. The crowd yelled for five minutes at the mention of this self-denying ordinance.[12]

How greatly the socio-religious issues and the problem of the Klan had lacerated the vitals of the Democratic party appears in certain of Franklin D. Roosevelt's *Papers*. Shortly after Davis' defeat in November, 1924, the future President sent to all the Madison Square Garden convention delegates an appeal for a diagnosis of the party's ills. The replies are illuminating. Some of them discussed "the religious issue"; more often Roosevelt's attention was directed to a larger complex of problems bedeviling the party. Many saw their party imperiled by Tammany, by the ambition of the Irish and of the newer immigrants for office, and by those forces that were associated with the newer America. There was little optimism expressed for 1928, and there were suggestions that the Donkey ought to learn from the Elephant the means of side-stepping such emotion-packed issues as those mirrored by the Klan. According to Representative Henry T. Rainey of Illinois:

We underestimated the strength of the Klan. This issue was loaded with dynamite. Republican leaders handled it diplomatically. In the campaign which followed the convention we exploded the dynamite contained in these propositions at every opportunity. We therefore lost the Klan vote.

There are more members of the Klan in the Democratic party than in the Republican party, and there are more Catholics in the Democratic party than in the Republican party. Therefore the deliberate injection of this issue into National politics assumes the proportions of a political crime, and the candidates and leaders who were responsible for it ought to be eliminated as much as possible in the future from active participation in party leadership.

Rainey was pessimistic:

Our present leaders stand first of all for the "Spoil of the Cities"—42,000 places in Chicago, 20,000 places in Indianapolis, 60,000 places in New York. In order to do this they must be,

(a) "Wet"
(b) Actively pro-Catholic, and actively anti-Klan
(c) Actively opposed to restricted immigration.

Query can we ever win under leadership which is compelled to accentuate these propositions?[13]

A sense of basic and insoluble dilemma pervades some of the letters. A midwestern lawyer thought fair play called for an effort "so far as possible, [to] nationalize Al Smith . . . who is entitled to the confidence of the Democratic Party." He noted that Davis' defeat had not prevented Smith from winning another great gubernatorial victory in 1924 and this raised serious doubts that he could be denied the nomination in 1928. The same midwestern Democrat confessed to occasional thoughts that the party

... could do no greater service to the country than by nominating Al Smith and discovering whether or not the public is able to forget religious bigotry in a national election. It might be worth while to suffer defeat in this cause.[14]

The letters which Roosevelt received from the delegates who sat through the sad days at Madison Square Garden are full of lamentations, although some took comfort even then in the thought that a man with the culture and background of Franklin Delano Roosevelt could conceivably allay the fears and bridge the gap between the two wings of the party. Much of the foreboding by the non-eastern delegates was caused by concern and dislike for the influence of the urban, machine-run, and non-Protestant element in the party. Though there was fervent hope that what had happened at the convention belonged to history, there was fear that the party was in for a time of troubles. Among delegates outside the Northeast the thought was expressed that the only way to exorcize the evil spirit of the alien eastern influence represented by Smith was to allow it full rein in 1928. This, of course, suggested a tacit willingness to accept the nomination of Smith. Some advanced a fair play argument that Smith was entitled to the nomination. Others were unimpressed and unwilling to trade what they considered a slight chance of success with Smith for a real prospect of victory with a more representative American ticket.

Even in the discouragement of the 1924 campaign

Democratic leaders were oppressed by the seemingly unavoidable prospect of another titanic and destructive struggle between McAdoo and Smith in 1928. It appeared that only some unforeseen circumstances, such as a failure of leadership on one side, could prevent it. After decisive victories in New York in 1924 and 1926, Governor Smith's prestige in the party soared to new heights. As the future would show, neither his religion, his Tammany connection, his opposition to the Eighteenth Amendment, nor the combination of these would be enough to block him.

If the Protestant, rural, and dry forces in the party had had bold leadership, possibly the result would have been different. For whatever reasons, McAdoo, after the exhausting struggle with Smith in 1924, failed utterly to fill the role of such a leader. Unless his belated backing of Senator Thomas J. Walsh early in 1928 be counted an exception, he did nothing to help transfer his role to another; his part, in fact, strongly suggests the behavior of the opossum. Perhaps he was convinced that nothing could stop the relentless march of the Smith forces.* Whatever the reasons for McAdoo's withdrawal from an active, open role in national politics, his absence was no guaranty of smooth sailing for the New York Governor. True, the collapse of McAdoo's leadership reduced the danger of another suicidal con-

* It is possible that some fresh light on McAdoo's inaction will appear when his papers are made generally available, but the facts seem plain without them. Democrats who were opposed to the nomination of Smith were in constant and worried correspondence, but during the important period, 1925-1927, McAdoo's political intentions remained obscure.

vention though it did not insure Smith's nomination in 1928. The choice of New York's Governor became more likely, of course. But even though Smith were to become the nominee, the odds would favor almost any Republican who might be named to oppose him. It now appears that some great dislocation, such as the Crash and Depression that came fifteen months later, was needed to make Smith the probable winner in November.

To millions of Americans Smith's vigorous opposition to Prohibition was a defiance of the Supreme Law, human and divine; yet it was precisely this stand that helps explain his great hold on the cities of the Northeast. Without the electoral votes of that section there could be no hope of victory in 1928. The Volstead Act was far from discredited in other sections, and this issue became the chief focus, at least openly, of the attack on the New York Governor. Had Smith been an Episcopalian rather than a Catholic and a product of Hyde Park rather than of New York City, his nomination would have been less terrifying to millions, but he would still have remained vulnerable in the South and West. For Prohibition was in large measure the culmination of a moral and religious crusade which was geared to a great commitment on the part of the majority of the evangelical Protestant churches. Since this is indisputably true, it is inaccurate and unfair to attribute all, or even most, of the opposition to the New York Governor to his religion. But Smith's social and religious orientations made his opposition to the Eighteenth Amendment even more obnoxious to many Americans whose heritage was strikingly different. There is a convincing body of evidence that the very thought of the wet cause led by a New York Catholic magnified Smith's religion, and the cultural complex of which it was a part, into a large menace. Those who had an ingrained conviction that Catholicism could not be other than an abiding challenge to American institutions were often the same men and women who were stanch advocates of Prohibition.

And so two issues, Catholicism and Prohibition, each with many overtones and neither typical of the great campaign problems of American national politics, became increasingly related as the 1928 campaign approached. Their intermingling defies anything like precise statistical analysis, but some sense of their interplay is important if we are to appreciate the oblique ways in which the religious issue affected the minds and emotions of American voters. The picture included more than these two issues. In the most profound sense, the intensity of the fight to prevent the nomination of Smith measured the strength of an older and rural-minded America for continued dominance over the newer forces which were concentrated in the large cities. In the urban centers were millions whose roots in the United States did not antedate the mid-nineteenth century but who were bent on social and political fulfillment. Achievement of the presidency or even nomination to that high office by one who represented the newer population groups would be a symbol of attainment for them all.

Within this broader setting the Prohibition and the

religious issues are only partly distinguishable. Certainly, it is not possible to calculate the relative importance of these two issues by the volume of newsprint each inspired. The writer has been altogether convinced, chiefly by the striking contrast between the slight attention given the religious issue in the printed sources and the much freer discussion of it in private letters, that anti-Catholicism was indeed the silent issue in the national press and that it was very much more significant than the somewhat meager news or editorial space assigned to it would indicate. In April, 1927, and in September, 1928, and to a degree throughout the four campaign months, the religious issue as dramatized by Smith received top newspaper billing; but as the sequel will show, it required unusually dramatic events to accomplish this.* Though some writers and newspapers were frank in their references to the religious issue, the subject was not often or fully explored. A kind of unspoken taboo existed in this area where the hiatus between the ideal and the actual was so great. This is a fact that must be, and has not always been, weighed by those who have generalized on the relative importance of these two issues. Public discussion of the Catholic question was certainly limited by a widespread sense of delicacy and shame. No such barrier stifled the full, even though not always forthright, debate on the Prohibition issue. For, despite the jeers and sneers in the East, the Eighteenth Amendment was, at least in its

* April, 1927, brought Smith's "Reply" to Marshall (see Chap. 3) and in September, 1928, Smith chose to devote a major campaign speech to the religious issue.

earlier days, a great social experiment. In broad objective it was even a "noble"* experiment.

Less than a year after the Democratic debacle of 1924, articles on the religious issue began to appear in some of the leading general periodicals. The *Forum* published a series of articles on Catholicism in the United States. Catholic and non-Catholic writers contributed. In a foreword the editors lamented that for too long "it has been the consistent policy of politicians and journalists to keep religious questions out of politics and out of print" despite the fact that the Catholic church "has been the subject of a sort of backstairs controversy."[16] Calling for frank discussion, the *Forum* ran first an article by Michael Williams, brilliant editor of the new and liberal Catholic *Commonweal*. Williams asked non-Catholics to state their grievances against his Church. He condemned the fake revelations found in anti-Catholic literature and stressed the Americanism of the Church of Archbishop Ireland and Cardinal Gibbons.[17]

A few months later William Franklin Sands, also a Catholic and a "distinguished diplomat . . . of Maryland's colonial stock," stressed a different aspect of the problem. Unlike Williams, whose claim that the Declaration of Independence and the Constitution "sprang in large part" from the ideas of Catholic philosophers

* The precise language which Herbert Hoover used in his acceptance speech was often misquoted. His words were [italics mine]: "Our country has deliberately undertaken a great social and economic experiment, noble *in motive* and far-reaching *in purpose*. It must be worked out constructively."[15]

must have seemed preposterous to most Protestant readers, Sands expressed an appreciation of the non-Catholic point of view. But with an obvious reference to Communism he warned Protestants of the need to resist "the new barbarism of Eastern Europe." This called for positive religious belief, and he commended to all the study of Catholic theology and discipline. In a broad spirit aimed at genuine understanding, Sands had words of wisdom for Catholics and for non-Catholics. He was concerned because his fellow religionists were too much "absorbed in their own transformation into the body of the nation to know what was taking place in the minds of their neighbors." He was distressed because non-Catholics "do not stop to consider that certain phenomena which they, and also many Catholics, observe with distaste, have nothing whatever to do with the Catholic Church but are in fact isolated manifestations . . . of clinging racial tradition."[18]

Professor R. H. Dabney of the University of Virginia reminded *Forum* readers that both Queen Elizabeth and President Wilson had acted on the assumption "that the theoretical position of the Roman hierarchy and the actual position of many individual members of the Roman Church are two wholly different things." Elizabeth in the sixteenth century had entrusted her fleet to a Catholic in the hour of England's great peril. President Wilson had a Catholic private secretary, and though some professed to believe that Tumulty had leaked everything telephonically to the Vatican, the United States had not lost the war. Dabney concluded with words of advice to Protestants:

That Catholic priests would like to substitute their parochial schools for the American public schools, and would like to influence politics in many ways,—just as Methodists and Baptists have gone into politics to prohibit the drinking of beer,— is of course true. But it is also true that many Catholic laymen decline to follow their priests in such matters. Far more of them, however, will follow the priests, if angered by the rabid attacks of such organizations as the Ku Klux Klan. The way to make Catholics tolerant is for Protestants to be tolerant themselves.[19]

Dabney's was but one of many appeals for the only kind of tolerance likely to stand the test—one based on knowledge as well as good will.

Too often such pleas went wholly unheeded, and there was usually some event that served to replenish the propaganda mills of professional Catholic baiters. The dramatic and colorful Eucharistic Congress at Chicago in the summer of 1926 served this purpose fully until an even more dramatic event, the exchange between Smith and Marshall, occurred in the spring of the following year. Attending the Congress were many of the leaders of the Catholic church, in the full panoply of princes of the Church. Very prominent among them was Cardinal Bonzano, the papal legate. Stopping in New York en route to the Congress, the Cardinal was publicly received in City Hall by Mayor Walker and Governor Smith in the customary manner of recognizing a cardinal, including the kissing of his ring.* To

* "The Freethinkers Society" vigorously protested an alleged breach in sound church-state relations. "When the City Hall and the Great Aldermanic Chamber of the City of New York are temporarily converted into a Catholic Cathedral . . . it is an affront to our Civil Government. . . . This Republic does not recognize the Papal State nor The Pope at Rome."[20]

Catholics and to some Protestants, the Congress, culminating in the great moment of the celebration of the Eucharist by a million and a half devout Catholics, was a thrilling spiritual experience, the color and splendor of it beyond anything in the annals of the Catholic church in America. To some non-Catholics, however, the Chicago Eucharistic Congress was the stimulus to new outcries against the pope. The Congress was widely used in 1926 and even in 1927 and 1928 to fan the flames of intolerance; nativism was temporarily refreshed by it, conveniently so for the political timetable. A sample reaction appeared in an open letter in the Klan's *Kourier Magazine*. The Reverend George W. McDaniel, D.D., President of the Southern Baptist Convention, addressed Cardinal Bonzano on the subject of a repeated invitation by the Pope that Protestants return to Rome:

> Dear Mr. Bonzano: We have received your official invitation to return to the mother church and courtesy demands that we reply. We respectfully but flatly decline your invitation.
>
> . . .
>
> —Furthermore, we must decline your invitation because we are citizens of the United States and owe supreme and sole political allegiance to this country. Our government was founded by Anglo-Saxons but among all the cardinals who landed with you not one was an Anglo-Saxon.[21]

Governor Smith's personal files are replete with samples of broadsides, cartoons, and advertisements of anti-Catholic "literature," some of it distinctly pornographic.[22] Mailed to Smith from all sections of the United States, it differed little from similar materials which appeared in earlier phases of the anti-Catholic

The Fellowship Forum *carried this cartoon in its issue of September 15, 1928. The caption read in part: "The ill-fated Nobile Expedition to the North Pole, in which many lives were lost recently, was begun under the auspices of the papal blessing. Nevertheless, it failed completely, dismally and abjectly. Now the pope is sending another expedition—this one to the Election Poll."*

movement; some of it was a direct steal from the Know-Nothing days of the mid-nineteenth century. A considerable amount was in circulation as early as 1923-1924; by 1926 the anti-Catholic propaganda presses were in full motion, and though there is no way of actually calculating the total, the bulk product became enormous. It is doubtful, however, whether Smith and some of his close advisers appreciated the full extent of the approaching storm.

The Eucharistic Congress at Chicago served conveniently to excite the fears of those who were deeply troubled by what they regarded as indications of a new Catholic militancy. The Klan and Klan-minded organizations continued to shout defiance, but of perhaps greater importance were the activities of such anti-Catholics as Methodist Bishop Adna W. Leonard of Buffalo. As president of the New York Anti-Saloon League, Bishop Leonard objected to Smith's views on Prohibition and in a sermon before a Citizenship Conference at Round Lake, New York, made it clear that Smith's wetness alone would be sufficiently damning to exclude him from the White House. The Bishop's sermon had much to say about the silent issue, which now erupted into loud warnings. "No Governor can kiss the papal ring and get within gunshot of the White House . . . ," he warned.[23] Condemnation of Catholics for "ring kissing" was not new, but this symbolic act performed by Catholics when presented to a cardinal had been highlighted for Americans by the news reports of Cardinal Bonzano's visit. The precise significance of and national dangers inherent in "ring kissing" became once again a topic of warm discussion. To Catholics and to many reasonable Protestants, Governor Smith performed a symbolic gesture and nothing more in kissing the ring;* but to the unsophisticated, the sermon of Bishop Leonard conjured up the image of Smith as a likely tool of the Vatican. To the obstacle of Prohibition, the Bishop now added the barrier of religion.

Of course, there was insistence that religion *per se* was not an issue and that all that was at stake was the principle of the separation of the temporal and spiritual spheres. Much of what the Bishop said was a product of a religio-cultural theory which accepts as a truism that excellence resides within the confines of the Nordic, Protestant, English-speaking world. He issued a "call for Anglo-Saxon unity, against foreigners, particularly the Latins." He is reported to have announced that the United States is a "Protestant nation and, as long as the English language is interwoven with the word of God, America will remain Protestant."[25]

The address was not without repercussions.† *The*

* It was said that Calvin Coolidge, when lieutenant-governor of Massachusetts, had kissed the ring of Cardinal O'Connell at a Boston War Memorial mass, thereby "merely offering the usual tribute to high clerical office."[24]

† President James L. McConaughy of Connecticut's Methodist-founded Wesleyan University was one of many who found the Bishop's words unpalatable. McConaughy used the occasion of college opening to teach tolerance while condemning Leonard's proscription of the New York Governor. The Connecticut educator looked darkly, too, on the Bishop's call for organizations "designed to save America for Protestant domination. Personally, it seems to me un-American, unwise, and almost unchristian-like for a religious leader, be he even a bishop, to denounce the presidential aspirations

New York Times in an editorial entitled "A Methodist Pope" opined that Bishop Leonard had made "about as big a blunder as is possible for a church leader" to make, that of attempting to commit a church "to a political program of intolerance and proscription." The *Times* suggested that if any Protestant church were to raise this issue it must be done "under cover," but that "Bishop Leonard has rushed to the housetops to shout it." The Methodist leader was accused of violating the very principle which he had accused Catholics of infringing—the involvement of a church in political affairs:

> Whatever the political sins of the Catholic Church may have been in the past, they cannot be denounced by men who are at the same time imitating them. We have no established church in this country, and it is vain for Bishop Leonard to imagine that he can set up one. . . . we are sure that many even of his co-religionists will sense the danger of making new presbyter read too much like old priest writ large.[28]

The New York *World*, enthusiastically pro-Smith, made the most of the Bishop's sermon. This paper, with its galaxy of great writers, covered the Leonard episode under a page one headline, "Methodists Open War on Governor Smith." According to the *World*, the Bishop had shouted, "I am a 100 per cent, Anglo-Saxon. . . . We are keepers of the Constitution, of the flag and of American citizenship." He had warned that ". . . we will never surrender our priceless American heritage to the hands of the foreigners who trample on

---

of a great state governor simply because he is not a Protestant."[26]

An interesting Catholic view of the Leonard affair is an article entitled "More Rum, Romanism and Rebellion."[27]

our flag."[29] It is plain that the Bishop had an eye cocked in the direction of the cosmopolitan population of New York City. To the Methodist Bishop and the vast number of Americans who saw America in like perspective, the *World* recommended a more responsible attitude and that they "do not hit out recklessly against 'the Latins,' whom you describe as 'hordes of the least desirable nations [who] came here to down our government.'" It was suggested that clergymen ought not to compete in matters "so well managed by the Ku Klux Klan."[30] Governor Smith made no reply to the Bishop's blast. He continued to maintain silence in the face of similar attacks. According to the *World*, when he was informed of Bishop Leonard's remarks, he "merely smiled."[31] Friends of the Governor expressed satisfaction, however, that opposition to him on religious lines was "being forced into the open instead of pursuing the usual whispering campaign." This was viewed as a favorable omen, showing "panic has overtaken the forces of prejudice."[32]

The Bishop had his stout defenders. One contributor to the Letters column of *The New York Times* warned that cardinals are "princes" and that "kissing their rings is flunkeyism." He advanced the interesting statistical conclusion that no more than ten per cent of the Bishop's opposition to Smith was chargeable to religious prejudice; at least ninety per cent must be labeled "spirit of 1776." He thought church-state relations were such in this country that "forty or fifty years hence a Governor of New York who is a Roman Catholic can be elected President."[33] There were some among both Protestants and Catholics who found the Bishop's ideas intolerable and who concluded, inaccurately, that they represented the view of all Methodists. A Brooklyn citizen, tired of fine-spun statements, concluded simply that Methodists are "very wicked people."[34] A Methodist who tried "to remain a Christian when he fails in being a good Methodist" thought his coreligionists ought not to "wonder that the Methodist Episcopal Church is so universally accepted as an intolerant organization when a high official of that church exhibits such narrowness. . . ."[35] A New Yorker was sure that "hundreds of thousands of liberal Protestants," repelled by such examples of political activity by the followers of John Wesley, "would welcome an opportunity to vote for a Roman Catholic—or a Hebrew, or a Unitarian or a Universalist, or an agnostic, or an atheist. . . . "[36] The Methodist Building, newly erected in the nation's capital, became to some the symbol of undue pressures, especially in the cause of Prohibition. This structure, located but a stone's throw from the House and Senate, was pictured by wet Senator Bruce of Maryland as a "browbeating vatican which the Board of Temperance, Prohibition and Public Morals of the Methodist Episcopal Church has erected just across from the United States Senate Office Building. . . ."[37]

But by no means was all the anti-Catholicism of the twenties the work of Methodists. Other denominations had a part in activities or pronouncements which, whatever their merits, intensified religious controversy in a manner likely to affect politics. One such episode, a fairly illustrative one, grew out of a meeting of the Presbytery of New York City. Under debate was a resolution to instruct Presbyterian ministers to urge their congregations to take definite stands on a proposal for a referendum on the Volstead Act. In the warmth of the discussion, which was as "heated as a political convention," the remarks that made the headlines were those of Dr. Henry Sloane Coffin, president-elect of Union Theological Seminary. The real issue was not Prohibition, said the famed theologian, but whether the Presbytery had any business to meddle in politics. "I don't think this Presbytery should tell people how to vote. . . . That is what the Roman Catholic Church does. We Protestants object to this."[38] This remark brought sharp reactions. From Providence came an offer of five hundred dollars to the New York Presbytery if Dr. Coffin could prove his charge.[39]* The New York *Catholic News* referred its readers to Protestant sermons for examples of pulpit politics. Its editor noted the complaints of newspaper reporters that Catholic sermons were newsless whereas each Monday's paper described Protestant sermons which advised congregations "to take this or that stand on some political issue."[40]

As 1926 drew to a close, *The New York Times* published some thoughtful pleas for mutual understanding, two of them contributed by members of well-known southern families. Each stressed the tragedy of denying to an eminently qualified Catholic full opportunity to reach the presidency, and each deplored unsupported

* Dr. Coffin expressed no interest in the money nor in a controversy, but he did not withdraw his statement.

fears and assertions that a Catholic, however distinguished and patriotic his career, could not be trusted fully as President. Henry Breckenridge cited instances of great Catholics, including Chief Justice White, who had served the country with complete fidelity.

> Are Americans so timorous that they fear the weakness of their institutions, the feebleness of their spirit of independent patriotism to the point that a Catholic President could subvert their institutions if he would? Is it American to judge Alfred Smith's political availability by his religion? Is it American to demand loyalty and service from Catholics and proscribe them from high office because of religion? Can a national unity be built on such discrimination?[41]

R. H. Dabney of Virginia expressed the concern of many that if Smith were nominated, the religious issue might cost the Democrats southern electoral votes. Weighing the Governor's chances, and banking on southerners to remember "the evil days of Republican reconstruction,"* he was "willing to risk it . . . if a campaign of education were skillfully conducted. . . ." Dabney added a thought which in all fairness should be pondered even though the final words were to prove too optimistic:

> It is a mistake to brand Protestants who object to a Catholic President as mere fools and bigots. For, while a few of them do deserve such characterization, the majority have simply inherited their anti-Catholic feelings from the old days, when theological hatred was at its height, and could easily be shown that their fears are unfounded at the present time.[42]

* The reference to "the evil days of Republican reconstruction" is an example of one of the fading, but still not altogether negligible, motives soon to be enlarged upon in the effort to overcome the special drawbacks implicit and explicit in Smith's candidacy. Even Tammany was represented as preferable to the Republican party.

Governor Smith ignored the early protests against a Catholic in the White House—cries frequently embellished, like Bishop Leonard's, with sweeping harangues against foreigners. If the Governor had traveled widely throughout the United States, he would have been made more aware of the many signs that his religion was a major political liability. His awareness of this was probably less profound than that of his friend and supporter, Franklin D. Roosevelt. Smith, nevertheless, must have had some appreciation of the fact that although the religious issue was important in all sections, the relative ease with which it was handled in states like New York, where tickets were "balanced" by the inclusion of Catholic, Jewish, and Protestant candidates, was not typical of the problem or its solution in much of the United States.

Writers and politicians remained divided in their views of the relative importance of the religious issue. For example, George Fort Milton, editor of the Chattanooga *News* and a McAdoo backer, was convinced that with Smith the nominee the issue would be Prohibition, not religion.* Politicians would have to make the final judgment at the nominating convention, and for this very reason, they of all people could least afford to be self-deceived. Senator T. H. Caraway of Arkansas was one of the professionals whose views were not to prevail at the 1928 Democratic national convention. Two years before convention time he offered his opinions to

* Milton predicted that if Smith were nominated a third party would be formed in the South and West with the result that the Governor would be beaten.[43]

the press. He felt that the recent Eucharistic Congress, the spectacle of cardinals in "sumptuous passage across the country in a monarchical train," tended to revive old suspicions. "If Governor Smith were a Baptist, a Methodist or a Presbyterian, he could be elected President of the United States. . . ."[44] To this the Jesuit weekly *America* expressed the hope "that the Senator is in error, and while we should not value at a high rate the chance of any Catholic candidate in certain remote and illiterate sections of the country, we believe that he is."[45]

CHAPTER THREE

The Marshall-Smith Exchange

> ... I join with fellow Americans of all creeds in a fervent prayer that never again in this land will any public servant be challenged because of the faith in which he has tried to walk humbly with his God.[1]
>
> —Alfred E. Smith

Long before 1928 the very thought of the nomination of Governor Smith for President had become an obsession in the minds of many Americans. Among those who regarded Smith as some sort of an incarnation of Sin were great numbers of men and, by all circumstantial evidence, even more women, who commonly took little interest in politics.

Haunted by the Democratic nightmare of 1924, some erstwhile McAdoo leaders found their way to the Smith camp in the hope of party peace or personal preferment. For millions of Democrats in the more rural parts of the United States, however, harmony and a possible Democratic victory would be a dreadful thing if the price were victory for "Al(cohol)" Smith and his Tammany, Catholic, liquor, New York crowd, to use some of the milder characterizations. In the South most Democratic leaders opposed Smith's nomination. In this they were in harmony with the collective moral judgment of the dry, Protestant church members of the South. Most of the Democratic leaders in the South were careful, however, to avoid an intransigent stand before the convention met in 1928, lest the move to block Smith fail.

The picture in the Middle West, especially in the more rural areas, differed little in this aspect from that of the South. As Senator Norris discovered to his sorrow, some Nebraskans opposed Smith because he was a Catholic as well as a wet. Was there a way out, without denying to Catholics their constitutional rights? Novelist Meredith Nicholson of Indiana, thinking he saw one, called for the withdrawal of all Catholic candidates. Like most Americans who inclined to this idea he lacked the temerity to suggest that a constitutional barrier already existed; but he feared that if a Catholic were nominated, "the ensuing campaign would develop a bitterness much like that of a civil war." *America* refused to concede that Nicholson's suggestion entailed no constriction of constitutional rights:

... Mr. Nicholson is no bigot .... What is to be thought of his proposal?

This Review observed some three years ago, after the hurly-burly of the Democratic National Convention had subsided into comparative sanity, that Catholics could see no particular advantage in having one of their number President of the United States. It repeats that observation now. There is nothing that Catholics could ask from a Catholic in the White House that they would not demand from a Jew, a Methodist or an atheist, for all they wish is a fair field and no favor.

Why, then, if Catholics have nothing to gain from a Catholic

President, should not some Catholic body authoritatively approve Mr. Nicholson's suggestion?

The case is not so simple. Catholics, as a body, have never taken part in a political campaign, and have sedulously avoided anything like the formation of a Catholic party. It is not wise to abandon that policy.

In the next place, such an approbation would be equivalent to an approval by Catholics of a religious test for Federal office.

Putting the matter in another way, Catholics would do what the framers of the Constitution carefully avoided doing.

In our judgment, Mr. Nicholson's well-meant plan is not only an invitation to bigotry to go a little further, but an attack upon the Constitution itself. We like the idea of requesting a Catholic to cede a constitutional right, simply because he is a Catholic, as little as we like the idea of asking a Methodist to withdraw simply because he is a Methodist.[2]

There was a marked increase in interest and concern about the "Catholic Question" in the summer and fall of 1926. By the first half of 1927 that interest multiplied, exploding finally onto the front pages of the nation's newspapers. With the exception of the Eucharistic Congress in Chicago in mid-1926, no incident in recent American history appeared to carry enough momentum to last through the 1928 campaign. Extremist organs like the *Kourier Magazine* of course kept up an anti-Catholic barrage, but more respectable publications assigned little space to the religious issue. This was generally true up to 1927, but in the first months of that year the dramatic focusing on the time-honored topic of dual allegiance brought the subject of a Catholic President to the attention first of periodical readers, then of serious newspaper readers throughout the United States. The big event came in April, 1927, when the

Atlantic Monthly published a challenge to Governor Smith by Charles C. Marshall. The next issue of the *Atlantic* carried Smith's reply.

As background for this notable exchange we should first consider a slightly earlier discussion of the dual allegiance question in a Unitarian paper, the *Christian Register* of Boston. In a sense the *Register* prepared the way for the *Atlantic* articles. Its editor, Dr. Albert C. Dieffenbach, launched his attack by noting that Governor Smith had in effect announced his candidacy for the presidency in his Inaugural Address of January 1, 1927. This, said the *Register*, forced a full debate on the propriety of a Catholic's seeking the highest office in the land. Dr. Dieffenbach predicted that the debate would be "immediate and protracted." It would be on "the most difficult and delicate problem that has ever confronted the American people," for the subject was "the two opposite ways of taking your religion into the State." It is fair to label this the opening blast in the 1927–1928 high-level challenge to Smith, as a Catholic, to run for the presidency. Continued the *Register:*

> Let no one jauntily dismiss this matter as though it were of no importance. Let superficial and fatuous talk about religion not having anything to do with politics be gone from this time forth. Let not the generous appreciation of Governor Smith (in which we share most heartily, for he is a remarkable person and a great statesman, for all his lack of erudition and refinement)—let not this feeling divert one from the weightier matters of the law of his Church and its aspirations to power clearly set down under official imprimatur in Catholic books that all may read. By all means let no one get excited or ill-tempered. Never was there a time when the decencies and amenities of our democratic life, in its pure devotion and re-

spect for every man and every faith, were called upon to serve the national well-being as they are called for now.

This is a time of dispassionate, but none the less thorough analysis of the whole religious situation. It is coming quickly to a head, be very sure, and we agree entirely with a broad-minded priest, the famous former army chaplain, Father Francis P. Duffy of New York City, that we face more than a number of specific religious questions, we face "a state of mind not uncommon among Protestants" toward the Roman Catholic Church. He has just replied to a remarkably plain letter on the subject, written from the enlightened Protestant point of view, by the distinguished Rev. Dr. Alfred W. Wishart of Grand Rapids, Mich., who, in *The New York Times* of December 26, 1926, says,—

"In short, we may as well face the issue. Before the class of intelligent and fair-minded Protestants I have in mind can be mentally at peace on these issues, they will want to know whether an American Catholic Presidential candidate endorses the claim of the Papacy to temporal power, its toleration, not its acceptance, of American principles, its attitude toward American public schools, and its rejection of the claims of millions of American Christians to *the right of self-government in religion* [our italics], as well as in politics."[3]

The *Register* pointed out that Catholics were expected to give allegiance to the "ideal" of a "Catholic state" and that this was bound to stir suspicion. It warned that the implications of the past summer's Chicago Eucharistic Congress had intensified Protestant suspicions. Catholics, wrote Dr. Dieffenbach, now had a unique opportunity.

It is our deliberate and calm judgment that the Roman Catholic Church, which, as Father Duffy says, is "an ancient institution and a very wise one," would do well to "reconcile herself with national or patriotic sentiment." Now is the opportunity. This is no time for plunging this country into a controversy the consequences of which might be catastrophic, for, with all our advancement in intelligence, the unpleasant fact remains that in religious issues the mass of people feel rather than think. They have emotions nurtured by centuries of faith, habit, and sentiment. Their religion is the most important factor in their conduct and character. It will come out with all might and intensity if this campaign persists. It is no more possible to confine the issues to economics, politics, and social welfare than it would be to denature the people of that which is the very center of their beings, even their religion. Governor Smith should renounce his ambition.[4]

Several days earlier Father Duffy had made an interesting comment on anti-Catholicism in this country in the light of European experience:

It is a queer thing, but the suspicion of the fundamental loyalty of Catholics is much more vivid in this country, where we think of ourselves as starting all over fresh and new, than it is in the older countries where Protestants and Catholics, three or four hundred years ago, fought fiercely with each other, using every weapon of warfare and persecution. The Swiss never doubt the loyalty of the Catholic cantons, which, by the way, have rather set the pace in devotion to country. Holland had a Catholic Premier some time ago, and the Prince of Orange did not quit his grave. Germany elected von Hindenburg over a Catholic, but there was little religious argument in the election. France has a Protestant President, but nobody is disturbed by it.[5]

Such a pragmatic approach to the problem had no appeal for Dr. Dieffenbach. Two weeks after its first warning the *Register* explained some of the special obstacles that would lie in Governor Smith's path should he choose not to accept Dieffenbach's advice that a patriotic Catholic must resist any temptation to seek the presidency. It published the results of a poll of non-

Catholic religious editors, who were asked to answer two questions:

I. Do you believe that a devoted Roman Catholic could serve as President of the United States in unqualified loyalty to the avowed American principle of the equality of all religions before the law, and at the same time in unqualified loyalty to the avowed Roman Catholic doctrine of the relation of church and state?

II. Do you believe that the frank discussion of the religious issue involved in Governor Smith's candidacy would serve a good purpose at this time?

Though it is not safe to assume that the views of an editor of a denominational paper always reflected those of the majority of those enrolled in his denomination, the replies are illuminating. The editor of the *Reformed Church Messenger* thought that if Smith ran:

. . . it is difficult to see how a frank discussion of this issue can be avoided, even if it subjects the Protestant press to the charge of bigotry. . . . It is quite likely that, with the recrudescence of sectarianism since the World War, the nomination of a Roman Catholic for the Presidency would precipitate a campaign of unprecedented intolerance and ill will. . . . The record of the Roman Catholic Church, in the claim of the Papacy to temporal power, the attitude toward the public school system, and the apparent autocratic rejection of the claims of millions of American Christians to the right of self-government in religion as well as in politics, makes membership in that organization a tremendous liability for any one who aspires to high political preferment. I think I can understand the fear of a possibility of papal domination, and what it might mean for our country—for example, in such a case as the Mexican situation—if the President of the United States were so obviously a man of divided loyalties. Constitutionally, we should not oppose any man because of his religious faith; and yet it seems justifiable to many broadminded Americans to question the propriety of having a representative of the Roman Catholic hierarchy in the White House.

Some of the Methodist and Baptist responses expressed the view that Prohibition was at least as important as religion in explaining why many Protestants could be expected to withhold support from Governor Smith. The majority of the editors replied in words not markedly different, in their effect, from those of the editor of the *United Presbyterian*, who acknowledged:

> If the choice were between a Roman Catholic and a Protestant, I venture that United Presbyterians would be quite unanimous for the Protestant. My own feelings are strongly against a Romanist for president.
>
> But in this particular case, there are so many other things to prejudice against Governor A. E. Smith, especially his attitude on prohibition, and his political associates, that I believe all church people should be warned against him, that he ought to be vigorously opposed, not on religious grounds only, but that the whole case against him should be stated.

Perhaps this will serve as an illustration of the much-repeated statement that Smith ought not to be opposed for the presidency merely because he was a Catholic.

A different kind of response came from the editor of the *Christian Leader* (Universalist, Boston):

> The second part of your question ignores the tremendous modification of Catholic theories which has taken place in the United States through contact with our ideals and institutions. Whatever power the Pope may have theoretically, he is too wise to use that power so as to cause a break with the Catholic Church in this country. Any attempt to give orders or bring pressure to bear on a Catholic President, Chief Justice, or Governor would be resented and resisted. American Catholics can

be good loyal citizens. How do we know? Simply by looking about us and noting the fact that they are.

Do I believe that a frank discussion of the religious issue involved in the candidacy of Governor Smith for the Presidency (if such a candidacy exists) will do good or harm? Both. Religious passions will be aroused. Bitterness will be stirred up. Should Governor Smith therefore refuse to run? No. Infinitely more harm would be caused by evading the question. We have a clear-cut issue of right and wrong. Are Catholics equal to the rest of us before the law? Is the principle of a square deal for everybody sound? Must any door of opportunity be closed to any American group because of race, or religion? Are Catholics entitled to be tested and tried by what they are and what they can do, like the rest of us? To evade this issue is cowardly. It is time to stand up and be counted for fundamental Americanism.[6]

Wilfred Parsons, S.J., editor of *America*, was incensed by what the poll revealed. After taking basic exception to its two questions on the ground that their framer "cannily refrained from indicating what he considered to be 'the avowed Roman Catholic doctrine of the relation of church and state,' " Parsons expressed his own conviction that these editors fairly reflected "the level of intellectuality, citizenship and Christian charity in those denominations." He thought that most of them would have to write an affirmative reply to a third question which was not expressly put to them: "Do you believe that the provision of the Constitution of the United States which states that no religious test shall be required of Federal officers should be repealed?"[7] The title of Parsons' article was a challenging three-word question: "Are Protestants Americans?"

The published results of the *Register*'s poll of Protestant editors created a stir, but it was very mild compared to the response to the two articles which appeared not long after in the *Atlantic*. The first of these was by Charles C. Marshall, a New York lawyer who had a considerable knowledge of canon law, though the profundity and accuracy of it soon became a matter of dispute. The title of his article, "An Open Letter to the Honorable Alfred E. Smith, A Question That Needs an Answer,"[8] was set in bold type on the *Atlantic* cover. The second and even more newsworthy article was by Alfred E. Smith, entitled "Catholic and Patriot: Governor Smith Replies." Editor and publisher Ellery Sedgwick accorded this article top-of-cover bold print notice and introduced the exchange by calling it "an historic incident, historic for the country and for the Church."[9] Sedgwick, as befitted the editor of New England's most influential periodical, had used the right mixture of patience and insistence. Other editors, including Christian Herter of the *Independent*, had hoped for a Smith interview or an article on his religion.* It was Sedgwick

* From late January 1927 on, F. D. R. appears to have been the unenthusiastic intermediary in the effort of a number of editors to arrange an interview or extract a statement from Governor Smith that would put him on record in this controversy. Through an intermediary Christian Herter "submitted a memorandum" to Smith. "The Governor received it with anything but enthusiasm. His main points were that his religion was his own business; that Taft, a Unitarian, who didn't believe in Christ (even as good Unitarian [*sic*] myself I didn't argue this point with him) had not been quizzed on his religion; that, if he started to explain what he believed, his fellow-Catholics—particularly the ignorant ones—would think that he was apologizing instead of explaining and that he would lose their support which he could not afford to do."[10] In replying F. D. R. asked for "more time to think it over" but as his "snap judgment" wrote that, if he were Smith, he "would decline definitely to give any interview on my religion. . . . He is

who succeeded, perhaps beyond his highest hopes.* It was, indeed, one of the great journalistic *coups* of the decade. Sedgwick was flooded with letters and the circulation of the magazine jumped.† Of course no one who speaks, writes, or publishes on the subject of religious controversy can hope fully to avoid suspicion; Sedgwick was no exception. Everything which the writer has seen, however, is convincing evidence that the editor of the *Atlantic* was motivated by patriotic impulses and thoughts when he published Mr. Marshall's "Letter." Sedgwick also exhibited shrewd and far-sighted journalistic sense.‡

---

quite right in believing that his record and his oath of office speak better than any other statement." Roosevelt thought that if any article were to be written it should be from the pen of "some well known Protestant."[11]

* See Sedgwick's own account of the background for the Smith article. Sedgwick credits Mrs. Moskowitz, "who was the heart and soul of the Governor's campaign," for the decision by Smith to enter the fray. Of Marshall, Sedgwick writes, ". . . this gentleman, being a High Church Anglican, loved Rome as the Devil loves Holy Water."[12]

† The effect of the Marshall and Smith articles on *Atlantic* Sales is interesting. Marshall's article brought newssales figures from a net average of less than 30,000 to over 54,000. The figure rose to over 72,000 for the May issue which featured Smith's reply. It cannot be assumed, of course, that the sales success of a magazine depends wholly upon a single article no matter how arresting.[13]

‡ Sedgwick had long believed that Smith's nomination would force the religious issue into the open and that it was vital that it be debated on the highest possible plane. He did not make Marshall, whom he describes as "a high authority on ecclesiastical law," privy to his full purposes. In fact it appears that Marshall came to Sedgwick's attention rather accidentally. A leaflet by Marshall was brought to Sedgwick by a friend who had found it in church. From this came the invitation to Marshall to do the *Atlantic* article.[14]

Marshall's "Letter" broke no new ground in the centuries-old debate, but its timing was significant. Even those who rejected its argument conceded that it was a gentlemanly presentation of the case of those who were convinced that the safety of the United States precluded the election of a Catholic president. In publishing Marshall's "Letter" and the "Reply" by Smith the *Atlantic* may be credited with an important effort to elevate the level of the old debate. The wisdom of making the effort at all and the degree of its success or failure may be debated, but even the Jesuit paper *America* conceded that Marshall's "Letter" was a "comparatively cultured" statement.[15] That is more than can be said for most of the contemporary writing on the dual allegiance theme.

Though most of it bordered on the legalistic there were overtones of a broader and more general import in Marshall's "Letter" to Smith. It is clear that the Episcopalian lawyer was disturbed about the impossibility, as he saw it, of fully reconciling allegiance both to Catholic dogma and to the Constitution. He was concerned because the possibility of a Catholic President came at a time when, according to Marshall, the Catholic church showed new strength in this country. Marshall wrote Smith:

> . . . your venerable Church, which recently at Chicago, in the greatest religious demonstration that the world has ever seen, declared her presence and her power in American life. Is not the time ripe and the occasion opportune for a declaration, if it can be made, that shall clear away all doubt as to the reconcilability of her status and her claims with American constitutional principles? With such a statement the only question as

to your proud eligibility to the Presidential office would disappear, and the doubts of your fellow citizens not of the Roman Catholic Church would be instantly resolved in your favor.[16]

Marshall acknowledged Smith's tremendous appeal as a candidate, based on ability, personality, and record. It is not necessary to do more than list the other subjects covered in the "Letter." In the areas of education, marriage, the "Mexican situation" and, embracing them all, the alleged conflict between the Constitutional law of the United States and the Two Powers theory of the Church, Smith was repeatedly asked how, as President, he would reconcile opposites. Illustrations of conflict, sometimes taken from the sixteenth century, were cited. It is perfectly clear from the "Letter" that Marshall was convinced that Smith could not answer the queries in any satisfactory way. Yet it is important that the reader note that Marshall's question to Smith was a personal one—one that concerned his own conscience; at this point Smith was not asked to prove that the hierarchy of his Church would endorse his answer. Marshall's "Letter" unquestionably strengthened the convictions of some well-educated non-Catholics who needed little argument to confirm their general impressions that Catholics ought to occupy offices below the level of the presidency, only. The evidence is more than circumstantial that, through newspapers and private letters, Marshall's challenge reached even the less literate. That it came through in one-syllable words did not weaken the effect.

In publishing Marshall's "Letter" Sedgwick of course

hoped to draw a reply from Governor Smith. To do this it was necessary that Smith be persuaded that he ought to depart from his custom of ignoring all charges against his religion. Early in March Sedgwick asked Franklin D. Roosevelt's aid:

> I have been greatly affected by your arguments in behalf of Governor Smith for President, and still more by the truly admirable record of the Governor in office. If he is nominated, I expect to support him, but I believe that, before his nomination, it is really necessary for the country to arrive at a definite understanding regarding the claims which his Church makes which are or seem to be, in direct conflict with American principles.
>
> I hope you will give me the credit of believing that I write this letter without a trace of bigotry. As a matter of fact, there have been Catholics in my immediate family circle, and I am more naturally drawn to the Roman Catholic Church than to any one of the Protestant sects, but I have been impressed with the definiteness of Papal assertion in matters of vital interest to a self-governing people.[17]

Sedgwick estimated that seventy per cent of the *Atlantic* subscribers were Republicans; he did not expect the majority of its readers to favor Smith for President. He was concerned about the religious issue in the campaign, first, because he felt that the American people were entitled to an affirmation by Smith that, as President, his Catholicism would in no way reduce his freedom as an American; and, second, he believed that "the real obstacle to his success in November is neither Tammany nor anti-Volsteadism, but simply the well-nigh universal fear among Protestants of the Catholic Church." Sedgwick believed this fear was being driven underground because the "church is becoming an

American Church. . . ."[18] Neither Roosevelt nor Smith was enthusiastic about Sedgwick's plan. The future President wrote a confidential letter to Smith, enclosing a draft of what he dubbed Marshall's "somewhat sophistical article" and he assured Smith of Sedgwick's high intentions and lack of bias. He found the whole business distasteful, but, knowing that Sedgwick was about to print the Marshall "Letter," he exerted his best efforts:

> . . . the Atlantic Monthly is pretty widely quoted and what amounts to a demand for an answer will cause a repetition of the questioning in many other publications and in the minds of a great many perfectly sincere people who ought to be on your side.

The silent treatment was, under these circumstances, judged not adequate to meet the Marshall challenge. There was some thought of entrusting an answer to a Protestant, possibly Roosevelt himself, but this idea was rejected on the ground that no reply by a Protestant could possibly dispose of the question of personal allegiance which Marshall had directed to Smith alone. As Roosevelt wrote to Smith:

> I am inclined to think that if an answer is made by a Catholic it ought to be gone over pretty carefully first with some broad-minded Protestants who are capable of judging the effect on Protestants.
>
> When all is said and done, the boldest, and, therefore, the most effective way of dealing with this whole situation would be for you to answer it yourself. You can do it in such a way that people all over the United States will respect you even more than they do now, just as your handling of the possibility of your presidential nomination in 1928 in your inaugural address won many to you because of its direct simplicity. Anyway, write me what you think. I am not writing to Ellery

Sedgwick until I hear from you, but I shall have to tell him something.[19]

Both Roosevelt and Sedgwick were quite aware of the portentous nature of the *Atlantic*'s venture. Roosevelt's intuitive political sense was alert to its explosive possibilities. Pressed by Sedgwick for some quick word from Smith, he again deplored the need for any reply at all.

. . . It will stir up discussion on religious issues which is not for the good of the country, particularly at a time when the animosities of the K.K.K. and the bitter feeling engendered at the last National Convention appear to be rapidly dying out.

That "open letter" is essentially legalistic. As a lawyer I could make it even stronger by going back a little further in the history of the Roman Catholic Church and quoting from Bulls of ancient Popes which would appear even more ridiculous to 20th century eyes. If I were to answer the letter personally I should do so in a humorous vein by quoting certain Unitarian ecclesiastical dignitaries to prove that Unitarianism is not Christianity and that, therefore, President Taft was not even a Christian. Further, I could easily quote from the sayings of individual Episcopal or Baptist or Presbyterian luminaries to prove that Wilson, Roosevelt, McKinley and Cleveland were, as members of various churches, secretly obligated to put the church ahead of their oath of office.

If the Article is answered at all it ought not to be answered, of course, by a Protestant, for such answer would carry little weight. If I were a Catholic I shouldn't answere [*sic*] it either, because I can't see the point of discussing 50 year old dicta of Pius the Ixnth [*sic*] in relation to American public officials of 1927 who happen to be Catholics. The point—the only point, and the whole point—to consider in regard to Governor Smith as Assemblyman, as Sheriff of New York, and as four times Governor of New York, and as a possible nominee for the Presidency, is the simple question, "Has he, as a public servant, ever allowed officials of his Church to dictate to him against public interest of the State?" The answer to that is of course a clear "No!", and his appointments, his building up of the public school system, his complete divorcement of any association between church and state must and do furnish the proof. He has lived up, not merely to the letter, but to the very spirit of his oath of office.[20]

While Roosevelt was expressing his strong distaste to Sedgwick, Smith pondered his own course with misgivings. He was far from being an expert on the dogma of his Church; he was, in fact, not very informed on the subject and thought that his public career was the best and only sensible answer to Marshall's question. But if tempted to ignore the matter altogether, the Governor was persuaded that there was in the challenge of the *Atlantic* article a special urgency, and perhaps a unique opportunity. The advice of very close political intimates, Mrs. Belle Moskowitz and Judge Joseph M. Proskauer, was apparently similar to Roosevelt's warning from Warm Springs. Whatever may have been the clinching argument, Smith agreed to answer Marshall in the May issue of the *Atlantic*.

Father Duffy, famed chaplain of the 165th Regiment in World War I, contributed much of the dogmatic argument, of which Smith was quite innocent. Judge Proskauer, an intimate personal and legal adviser to Governor Smith, also had a very important part in the preparation of the "Reply." Smith's freely admitted ignorance on matters of dogma should have counted naught against him, for it will be recalled that Marshall's challenge was a very personal one: Could Smith as a Catholic uphold the Constitution under all circumstances? The query may have lacked contact with reality; but unless answered to the liking of the suspicious, it could, even if he were nominated, almost certainly defeat him in the fall election, assuming defeat did not come as a result of other factors.

To say that Smith's "Reply" to Marshall was eagerly awaited is to understate the case. The article, not yet ready for release, and apparently in imperfect form, was physically appropriated by a representative of the Boston *Post* while "visiting" the *Atlantic*'s printing establishment. Sedgwick was called from bed by news of the illegal seizure and of the *Post*'s intent to print Smith's "Reply" in advance of the authorized release date. He was obliged to rush this number of the *Atlantic* by special trucks to New York, where certain other newspapers had followed the high-handed example of the Boston *Post*. This skulduggery did not succeed in spoiling Mr. Sedgwick's *coup*. On the composition of the Smith article as well as the theft of it Sedgwick writes:

> The week that followed was in his contemplative years a source of much merriment to Al Smith. What had he to do with ecclesiastical polity? He was American to the last drop of his blood. He was Catholic heart and soul. He loved his country and he worshipped God. When these simplicities became involved in ecclesiastico-political argument, it was all beyond him. His action at the time was to summon his Board of Strategy—priests and professors—men learned in law and history, politicians who had been born the day before yesterday and never in all the years taken their eyes from the political football. They wrote the article, rewrote it, scrutinized every sentence with a magnifying glass, and then Governor Smith studied it just as he used, when a boy at the parochial school, to study the ultimate intricacies of Aquinas and Jerome

brought down to school level. With a touch here and there he put Al Smith into all of it and made it his very own.

The riot of excitement that article caused! Hardly a daily paper in the United States but reprinted it. It led to theft and injunctions and a complicated lawsuit (which it gave the editor huge satisfaction to win),* and it sent off Governor Smith's campaign to a flying start.[22]

Smith met Marshall's challenge with a reply, the heart of which was in two very notable concluding paragraphs which appear below. The "Reply" gave Marshall the assurance that was, by the terms of the challenge, supposed to resolve doubts about Smith's fitness for the presidency. Smith answered Marshall, too, by asserting that Catholic authorities were quoted out of context, by insisting Marshall had taken his whole thesis from a "limbo of defunct controversies," by quoting from Archbishop Ireland and Cardinal Gibbons in praise of public schools and the separation of church and state in the United States, by rejecting as ridiculous the notion that each Catholic must defend every statement of every pope and prelate, and—most tellingly—by the pragmatic argument that the proof of the loyalty of Catholics to the United States was, as with Protestants, in the lives of people, including the record of the present Governor of New York. Most persuasive of all was the summary and conclusion of Smith's "Reply":

I summarize my creed as an American Catholic. I believe in the worship of God according to the faith and practice of the Roman Catholic Church. I recognize no power in the institutions of my Church to interfere with the operations of the

* Sedgwick sued the Boston *Post*. Mr. Sedgwick told the writer that the out-of-court settlement was in his favor.[21]

Constitution of the United States or the enforcement of the law of the land. I believe in absolute freedom of conscience for all men and in equality of all churches, all sects, and all beliefs before the law as a matter of right and not as a matter of favor. I believe in the absolute separation of Church and State and in the strict enforcement of the provisions of the Constitution that Congress shall make no law respecting an establishment of religion or prohibiting the free exercise thereof. I believe that no tribunal of any church has any power to make any decree of any force in the law of the land, other than to establish the status of its own communicants within its own church. I believe in the support of the public school as one of the corner stones of American liberty. I believe in the right of every parent to choose whether his child shall be educated in the public school or in a religious school supported by those of his own faith. I believe in the principle of noninterference by this country in the internal affairs of other nations and that we should stand steadfastly against any such interference by whomsoever it may be urged. And I believe in the common brotherhood of man under the common fatherhood of God.

In this spirit I join with fellow Americans of all creeds in a fervent prayer that never again in this land will any public servant be challenged because of the faith in which he has tried to walk humbly with his God.[23]

The newspaper reaction to Smith's "Reply" was overwhelmingly favorable to Smith, though some of the praise was too faint and perfunctory to count much for the campaign ahead. *The New York Times*' support was enthusiastic, the *Herald Tribune*'s was belated and skimpy. Both Marshall's "Letter" and Smith's "Reply" were printed in full or in large part by the great metropolitan papers. Much attention was directed to the final paragraph, which was Smith's *credo* as well as his personal answer to Marshall's question. These words expressed Smith's honest and heartfelt conviction.

The large newspaper spread given this compelling statement encouraged some to hope that the religious issue might be removed from the coming campaign altogether. At the very least it was hoped that Sedgwick had succeeded in raising the level and tone of the discussion. But while it is fair to assume that the Marshall–Smith exchange was calculated to serve this end, in the short run anything that called attention to Catholicism as an issue seemed inevitably to instill new vigor into the activity of the bigots.

No answer that a prospective Catholic presidential nominee could have made to the question Marshall asked Smith would have satisfied those who shared Marshall's fears. Some insisted that Smith's disposition of the historical cases cited by Marshall was marked by error and even by casuistry. While the evaluation of the dogmatic argument is beyond the scope of this inquiry, it is important to emphasize that after the publication of Smith's "Reply" the attack was shifted to new ground. This was done in an effort to show that in his answer to Marshall, Smith had overstepped good Catholic doctrine. If elected President, the argument ran, he would be likely to face interference from a hierarchy which it was assumed could not approve his independence and his invoking of conscience as the final arbiter in Catholic thought and action.

This shifting of ground was, of course, implicit in the whole attitude of all those Protestants, whether low evangelicals or High Church Anglicans, who were utterly convinced that Catholics, even in the twentieth century, might receive conflicting orders in matters affecting their highest duties as citizens. Perhaps the Smith strategy board should have seen this clearly and have advised the Governor to remain silent. However this may be and without implying insincerity, it should be remembered that it was Smith who answered in a forthright way the question put to him. Despite this, Marshall and his followers found it prudent to call that answer unsatisfactory.

Reader interest was very great. In its July number the *Atlantic* announced it had been flooded with letters. Sedgwick again explained to *Atlantic* readers that his objective had been to provoke serious and wider discussion and that this had been attained. He acknowledged that not everyone was satisfied that his motives were above reproach. Some charged a conspiracy. To them Sedgwick replied:

> . . . If ever there was an honest debate, honestly printed, it was the Smith-Marshall correspondence. Both gentlemen wrote with vigor and absolute conviction of their minds and hearts. The villainous statement, wherever made, that the debate was a pretense, framed by collusion in advance, is an unqualified falsehood, cruel to Mr. Marshall, whose whole life is a testimony to the sincerity of his convictions, libelous to Governor Smith, whose career has been lived in the calcium light of publicity, and insulting to the *Atlantic*.[24]

Marshall's "Letter" and Smith's "Reply" had come with dramatic force, but any appraisal of immediate profit or loss is an uncertain business. It would appear that, if the *Atlantic* had raised the level of discussion of the Catholic question, it had also unwittingly intensified the unbending determination of the intolerant. Many were convinced by the sincerity and simplicity of

Smith's "Reply" that the old debate over dual allegiance had lost its power. Some were sure, others hoped, that the religious issue had been largely removed from politics. These tended to underestimate the force of an old and tough tradition in our history which now took the form of a prompt insistence by skeptics that Smith prove that his *apologia* reflected the precise views of his Church's hierarchy. Small wonder that he refused to continue the controversy. Until after his nomination more than a year later, the Governor resumed his "no comment" policy.

CHAPTER FOUR

Enter Tom Heflin and Tom Walsh

> . . . If Al Smith wants to be elected president the ticket should be Smith for president and Heflin for vice-president, and let Heflin go over the United States villifying Catholics, and it would give Al the only chance in the world to be elected.[1]
>
> —George Fort Milton

Among those whom *The Catholic World* called ". . . the blusterers, the foamers at the mouth . . ."[2] none had the forum enjoyed by that caricature of Senator Claghorn, the frock-coated Senator Thomas J. Heflin of Alabama. Like some demagogues before and since, he was by none less appreciated than by many citizens of his home state. Heflin's anti-Catholicism was probably less provocative in the long run than the more subdued varieties of that malady. The junior Senator from Alabama unleashed a flood of bombastic and hate-inspiring speeches, many of them before the Senate of the United States. These speeches are a fair sample of the copious literature of extreme bigotry of the nineteen twenties. A few excerpts will illumine the quotation at the head of this chapter.

As Smith's prestige rose rapidly through 1927 and early in 1928, Heflin warned of coming doom. His haranguing was not confined to the South nor to the nation's capital, but the hall of the Senate provided the best opportunity for broadcasting his opinions of the Pope and of those who looked to Rome for spiritual guidance. Very early in 1928 Arkansas' Senator Robinson, soon to be Smith's running mate, complained that the Senate had been treated "a dozen times," in as many months, to Heflin's "anti-Catholic speech."

> I have heard him denounce the Catholic Church and the Pope of Rome and the cardinal and the bishop and the priest and nun until I am sick and tired of it, as a Democrat.

The *Congressional Record* reports this sequel:

> Mr. Heflin. "I would like to have the Senator make that speech in Arkansas."
>
> Mr. Robinson of Arkansas. "I will make that speech in Arkansas, and I will make it in Alabama, too."
>
> Mr. Heflin. "If you do, they will tar and feather you."[3]

Heflin insisted the "tar and feather" speech was meant as a joke. He had intended to delete the remark from the *Record* but weariness had prevented it.[4] He never ceased his vitriolic attacks on the Catholic church. One of his more serious charges was that the hierarchy hoped to send American boys to fight the Pope's battles in Mexico. If Heflin overreached himself in the "tar and feather" speech, he did not stay long abashed. If he did not range as widely as Huey Long a decade later—for Heflin interspersed no recipes for pot liquor—he did garnish his insults with occasional dashes of humor. He charged that the Democratic party had been shamefully and needlessly demoralized since 1924, the year in which Catholics had very nearly killed the party of Jefferson. Of the 1924 fiasco Heflin said:

> . . . John W. Davis—a very able, clever gentleman but the poorest politician that ever stood in front of a political army—permitted these gentlemen, not as Americans, not as Democrats, but as Roman Catholics, to insist that he denounce the Ku-Klux Klan and finish our chances of success at the polls after the convention had rejected that notion.
>
> Then they sent word to Mr. Coolidge, so it is said, to join Mr. Davis in denouncing the klan. A bunch of priests called on him and told him Davis was going to denounce the klan, it is said, and that he had better denounce it, too, and they would eliminate that question as an issue.
>
> Coolidge said he did not make a chatterbox out of his mouth about things that were not in the platform. [Laughter] And he got elected, the Senator from South Carolina [Mr. Blease] suggests. But what did John W. Davis do?
>
> Mr. Blease. "He got what he ought to have gotten; he got beaten."
>
> Mr. Heflin. "John W. Davis denounced it after this group of Catholics from Tammany, New York City, Al Smith's crowd, insisted that he denounce it, even after the great Democratic Party of the Nation had declined to take such action. Were they not putting the government of Rome above the Democratic Party then? Of course, they were; there is no other conclusion; and in an evil hour Davis denounced the klan and lost four States by that action."[5]

Heflin charged that a "Catholic Party" existed in the United States: "There are three distinct political parties in this country today—the Democratic Party, the Republican Party and the Roman Catholic Party."[6] Heflin told the Senators that such outstanding men as Lafayette,

This much-used cartoon piles up many objections to Smith's candidacy, among which the symbol of his religion is the only one left unlabeled. (New York State Library, Albany)

Herriot, and last but, in his list of statesmen, not least, Tom Watson of Georgia, had taken the same dim view of Catholicism as did the junior Senator from Alabama.

Heflin was indeed in the tradition of those demagogic diversionists who played on the fears and ignorance of the untutored. His stock in trade was the appeal to religious prejudice and racial fears. White women must be safe; Heflin offered lynching as the proper defense against rape. He castigated the New York *World;* he denounced the New York Congressional delegation for supporting antilynching legislation. "Choose ye this day whom ye will serve, the God of white supremacy or the false god of Roman social equality."[7] The reader will not miss Heflin's alignment of Catholicism with the nightmare of "social equality." On the whole, Heflin and the Heflinites probably influenced some voters, but ". . . the only thing which could make him . . . dangerous," in the opinion of *Commonweal*, "is the possibility that his present attitude in the Senate has been cleverly assigned to him by some forces which prefer to remain incognito."[8] *Commonweal* charged no such agency. Thinking people usually treated the Alabama charlatan as a disgraceful but still comic figure. When rumors spread that, in the event Smith were nominated, the Klan would nominate Heflin for President, expecting thereby to insure a Republican victory, *The New York Times* congratulated Smith on his enemies. Such a move by the Klan would, according to a *Times* editorial, "scare the life out of the Republican leaders about States like Pennsylvania, New Jersey and Illinois."[9] Actually, Heflin was never a serious political threat to the nation. Some may have supported Smith in part because of the demonstrable dangers of Heflinism, given rein. Fortunately the saving grace of humor often cut the Senator down to size. Soon after Smith's nomination the *New Republic* ran several "Premature Obituaries." One was of Heflin, exposing him as a Papal Legate, directed by Rome to overthrow the Ku Klux Klan. As the Papal armies landed in America, Tom Heflin murmured, "Now it can be told!" and expired.[10]

The importance of a phenomenon like Heflin, as distinguished from his color and ability to exasperate, is difficult or impossible to calculate. It is good to leave the mouthings of the most notorious of the Catholic-baiters in the *Congressional Record* and sample the expressions of people whose names are obscure but whose collective feelings were important. Some of these are registered in that excellent repository, particularly for opinion in the Upper South, the *Papers* of Josephus Daniels. Journalist and erstwhile member of the Wilson Cabinet, the North Carolina liberal was a man of great influence. He received and replied to questions on many subjects, including religion. "To settle a little dispute will you please write us if Mr. William G. McAdoo ever at any time belonged to the Catholic Church?"[11] So ran one husband-and-wife query in 1924.* There is no means of knowing whether, even then, thoughts of Al Smith inspired the question. In any event it was not a unique question.

A number of letters bespeak a revived interest in the

* Daniels settled the "dispute" by explaining that McAdoo had always been an Episcopalian.[12]

alleged pro-Catholicism of some of our former Presidents. Daniels found it necessary to assure a questioner that whatever contact President Wilson may have had with His Holiness was no more than formal. The provocative spirit behind such inquiries was almost surely the awful thought of Al Smith in the White House. The correspondence of southern and western politicians used by this writer contain many hundreds of insistent warnings in the half-decade before 1928 that no danger, nullification of the Eighteenth Amendment included, transcended political Catholicism. The warnings became far more frequent and urgent during and after the Marshall-Smith exchange. Southerners reared in the Jeffersonian tradition of freedom tried to remove the doubts of those who were deeply convinced that Protestants alone should grace the White House. Said Josephus Daniels:

> I do not believe that any Catholic ought to support Governor Smith and I do not believe that any Protestant ought to vote against him because he is a Catholic. Religious affiliations ought not to enter into the nomination or election of any public official.[13]

It would be agreeable to report that Daniels' injunction accurately represented the view of most of those who wrote him on the subject of religion. On the contrary, there were many, both lay and clerical, who felt no compunction in freely displaying their strong feelings against the Catholic church. In the great majority of instances the emphasis was on the political character of the Church, but there was derogatory comment about Catholic belief and practices. The more common complaint was that the Catholic church had limitless political ambitions and that its aims were in conflict with true American citizenship. A South Carolina minister warned that there were religious as well as social reasons for opposing Smith:

> By reason of his affiliations with a man in Rome, Italy, who claims to be political ruler of the whole world, he can hardly be a logical candidate for the presidency of the kind of government that has been established here. All we care for the claims of the pope is to oppose a system of government that has been discarded four centuries ago.
>
> The people are trying to say as little as possible but if ever they should be forced to it, forty thousand defenders of civil liberty will rise up all over this land.[14]

Despite the considerable evidence of strong anti-Catholicism in the South, there were grounds for the protests against the invidious charges that intolerance was a monopoly of any one section. Granted the South had a strong anti-Catholic bias, there is ample evidence of a like attitude in many parts of the North. It is true that nowhere in the United States was there more downright ignorance about the facts of Catholicism than was displayed in the South. On the other hand, some of the finest efforts to combat prejudice were made in that section. It remains true, however, that there was a vast reservoir of "No-Popery" spirit in the South and that much of it was extreme. Except in Louisiana and Maryland, Catholics in the South were greatly outnumbered by Protestants. In some remote areas there were people who had never seen a Catholic, much less talked with one.

Among the more intriguing letters of 1927–1928 are some written by northerners to southerners appealing to the sons and grandsons of the Confederacy to rescue the country from Al Smith. The nomination and election of Smith, so ran the argument, would saddle the nation with a wet, Catholic, Tammany government. The earnest message of a Vermonter to Daniels is a sample. It was essential to keep Smith within the confines of New York State, the plea ran, because his followers were:

> I. The "Tammany Hall" Democrats who want Tammany to rule over the country as he rules over New York City.
> II. The Wets, the whole Booze Gang who want the 18th Amendmt [*sic*] repealed and the old time saloon back again.
> III. The Roman Catholics who want the Catholic Church and the Pope to get a strong hold on our country through Al Smith's Appointments which they would dictate and which would be Chiefly Catholics. May the good Lord and the Southland keep us safe from the rule of the Wet, Tammany, Roman Catholic Booze Gang.[15]

Some New Yorkers, conceding the excellence of Smith's record as Governor, saw his religion as sufficient ground for a refusal to support him for the presidency. One of these, a Brooklyn resident, expressed it typically:

> Al Smith has made a very good concientious [*sic*] Governor in my estimation, but even Al . . . has his human limitations, and as the successor to Wilson, Cleveland, Roosevelt and our present incumbent, and I say this as a Democrat—Perish the thought!
> With Presidential power—what would he have done in the Mexican Crisis 8–10 months ago, with the K. of C. and other organizations bringing such pressure on him.
>
> . . .

As President—don't you think he would be subservient to however a small degree to the Pope in Rome—witness the kissing of the ring of the visiting Cardinals?[16]

Many westerners shared this aversion to Catholics. Their bias was sufficiently widespread to give point to southern resentment against the presumption that most of the intolerance could be found within the confines of the old Confederacy. Patrick Callahan, outstanding leader in the attempt to increase understanding between Catholics and Protestants, made the point with force and humor in an allusion to the unhappy state of mind of one of his salesmen, an Irish Catholic whose sales territory had been shifted from a very strong Klan state, Georgia, to Indiana. After a year the distressed paint vendor appealed to Callahan, "For God's sake take me away from those Northern Kluxers and send me back to Georgia!"[17]

As the "Protestant Crusade" gained momentum in 1927 and 1928, mounting tons of salacious and vulgar propaganda flooded the land. Time-honored accounts of horrors suffered by ex-nuns were republished and sold in bargain packets. Maria Monk, whose *Awful Disclosures* was the "Uncle Tom's Cabin of Know-Nothingism," was revived.* Though hoary with age, these stories were new to twentieth-century Americans and served the end of spreading suspicion. Perhaps more important than the brisk sale of bigoted books and

* Published in 1836 this fantastic and wholly disproved account of sexuality and murder at the Hotel Dieu Nunnery in Montreal, by a "nun" who was never there, early became the bible of anti-Catholicism. Three hundred thousand copies were sold before the Civil War, with numerous new editions and sales since 1865.[18]

pamphlets was the suspicion of Catholics voiced in publications written by and for educated people. *Commonweal* took notice of such sophisticated anti-Romanism, finding an example of it in the *New Republic.*[19] *Commonweal* noted that, though the *New Republic* applauded much of what Smith championed, it suggested that his religion raised questions so serious as to make him a dubious choice for President. The *New Republic* thought that any Catholic President would be subjected to Church pressure on two important and controversial current problems, education and the Mexican issue. It was not difficult to reply that on the public schools issue a clear verdict of innocence was implicit in Smith's long legislative record. On the second point, United States relations with Mexico, Governor Smith, of course, had had no opportunity to make a record.

Fears and half fears of this kind were certainly important in the anti-Catholic phase of the campaign of 1928, which was in middle gear many months before Smith was nominated. Cartoons served the purpose well, for they conveyed the mood of a secret conspiracy to invade Mexico, to close the public schools as well as Protestant churches, to burn Protestant Bibles, and to frighten the gullible with the bloody "oath" of the Knights of Columbus. It was suggested that pitted against so powerful and unscrupulous an organization as the Roman Catholic Church "President" Smith would be putty. There was undoubtedly in the thoughts of millions the lurking suspicion that not even Smith, whose conscience was, after all, Catholic, would or could resist a putative move by his Church to influence his decisions. This, of course, was no attack on religion; America was to be saved without so much as a whisper or an insinuation of criticism of the Catholic religion.

Early in 1928 there was a belated effort to challenge Smith's strategic position in the race for the Democratic nomination by entering Senator Thomas J. Walsh of Montana in a number of state primary races. The much admired Teapot Dome prosecutor entered the contest without bright prospects of overcoming the well-organized efforts of the Smith forces. Not only was Walsh a late starter, he also had the crippling disadvantage of residing in a state with few electoral votes. Despite this, a closer look at the Walsh candidacy has point.

Like Smith, Walsh was a Catholic. It is interesting that, as the election year opened, two leading candidates for the Democratic nomination were Catholic. Walsh was from a sparsely populated western state, was a strong dry and, of course, had no connection with Tammany Hall. For over a decade the Montana Senator had supported McAdoo, Smith's bitter opponent in 1924. The choice between a wet, Tammany Catholic, and a dry, rural Catholic suggested the possibility of a test to see whether Prohibitionist and Protestant Democrats, especially in the South, would support a Catholic who did not symbolize the wet, machine-run metropolis. Of course, the final test would come only in the event Walsh won the nomination. Walsh had many claims to party preferment. When his name was entered in several state primaries, there was satisfaction in some anti-Smith quarters that, if the Walsh campaign succeeded, dry Democrats who voted for him would prove their lack of religious prejudice while supporting an outstanding American for the highest elective office.

Walsh's excellent chairmanship of his party's tumultuous convention at Madison Square Garden had added to his renown as a prosecutor of the guilty in the Harding administration. It is probable that, at the beginning of his campaign, few knew that Walsh was a Catholic. Granting that Senator Walsh's religion did not intrude itself, there remains this more pertinent question: Would he not, as a candidate for President, have been subjected to attacks both by the bigots and by those who, like Charles Marshall, were troubled by the allegiance issue? Would not the challenge in Marshall's "Letter" have been applicable to any Catholic, including a dry, Montana Catholic? Some Catholics thought Walsh's candidacy would have a salutary effect. A pro-Smith Catholic editor, revealing no prophetic gift, wrote Colonel Callahan: "Walsh going in will keep all silent on the religious issue till after convention and many will remain silent then. He is making a great sacrifice for the good of us all."[20]

An attack on Walsh as a Catholic would surely have been made had he been nominated, but it is probable that the fear of Rome could not have been used as effectively against the Montana Senator as against Smith. Except in a most indirect and farfetched way, Walsh could not have symbolized, as did Al Smith, the insistent claims for more recognition of the newer and urban population groups. Admirers of Walsh were sure that had the Montanan been nominated, the religious issue would have played a much reduced role. At one time this was an opinion held by the Montana Senator himself. Midway between the 1924 and 1928 elections a Brooklyn Protestant clergyman who described himself "as one of thousands of your protestant admirers" wrote Walsh:

> . . . Ever since I have known you in public life my admiration of you as man and statesman has grown by leaps and bounds. We sometimes hear of the bugaboo of "religious prejudice" in political life. I know such talk is pure bunk, so far a [*sic*] really intelligent folk are concerned.[21]

Not yet disillusioned, Walsh replied:

> . . . I am quite in accord with you in the view that if any citizen should capture the imagination of the country and should exhibit the requisite capacity and devotion to the cause of the people, his religious affiliations would be no barrier to his selection. Opposition to him on that ground would, in my judgment, bring him as much support as he would lose.[22]

Long before convention time, 1928, there is evidence that many responsible leaders feared that if Smith were denied the nomination Catholics would attribute that failure to his religion. This concern was itself politically important. So, too, was the general attitude of discouragement among Democrats, and especially among anti-Smith Democrats, in the months before the party convention met at Houston. Among some highly placed party leaders there was a strong impression that in all probability 1928 would have to be sacrificed to the "Smith crowd." With so able a leader available, it was certain that the New Yorker's devoted backers would count religious discrimination as the prime reason should he fail to win the nomination. To escape this dilemma the Walsh candidacy appeared as a heaven-sent opportunity. As a government employee wrote to Daniels:

> Governor Al Smith of New York State, who is a Catholic and a "wet" looms large in the public eye as a presidential candidate. He leads the field of prominent Democrats. If he is not nominated as the Democratic candidate, it will take convincing considerations to satisfy Catholics that he has not been denied the honor because of his religion. That would have a serious reaction upon the Democratic candidate whoever he might be.
>
> Now, it seems to me that this situation can be avoided if Democrats who are not "wet" and not either Catholics or motivated by religious prejudice will make the effort.
>
> Senator Walsh of Montana who is a Catholic, is one of our most outstanding Democrats. If he were nominated, no Catholic could say that it indicated prejudice against his religion. I doubt if the "wets" would oppose him. Put a man like Hull of Tennessee on the ticket with Walsh, and it would be a ticket for which thinking Americans could stand with satisfaction. We would thus eliminate largely the "wet" and the religious issues, and at the same time get two of the best candidates the Democrats can produce. Think it over.[23]

Late in February, 1928, the indefatigable journalist Mark Sullivan had free advice for the Democrats:

> . . . I think there is now an opportunity to do a fine public service. I think Walsh of Montana ought to be put into the race. Among other wholesome advantages, it would provide two opportunities. It would show that not all the Catholics in the country are united behind any one candidate just because he is a Catholic; it would show that not all the Catholics are behind Smith. Second, it would provide those drys in the South, who are not actuated by religious prejudice, with an opportunity of demonstrating that they are willing to get be-

hind a Catholic, regardless of his religion, provided he is dry. . . . Walsh has a constructive mind. . . . He functions in the world of reason.

. . . I have never had a political hunch that struck me stronger than this one that Walsh should now be thrust into the race.[24]

Despite the very high regard in which he was held by politically conscious and educated Americans, there were overwhelming obstacles in the path of those who wished to implement their convictions that Walsh would make a fine President. The memory of the man in the street was short, and Tom Walsh had but a small fraction of the emotional impact of Al Smith. Walsh had numerous political liabilities. Most painful and ironical was the considerable abuse he suffered for contesting with another Catholic for the nomination. And, as a long-time McAdoo supporter, he was denounced as a mere stalking horse for the Ku Klux Klan! Walsh was indignant on both counts, but he appears to have been dealt a crippling blow by the pro-Klan charge in California, the key state contest for delegates.* He resented the charge that his continuous support of Mc-

* After Walsh's defeat in the California primary, J. T. Carroll, a political supporter, wrote him that the explanation was largely "too much McAdoo. . . . Too short a campaign. . . . Religious prejudice." Elaborating on the last of these the supporter said, " 'Twas easy enough to line up the ministers, but when it came to casting a vote for a 'horrible catholic' many of the laity rebelled." Unauthorized cartooning of Al Smith as a "drunken bum" seems to have backfired. Carroll was one of those who remembered Walsh's services in the Harding administration. He quoted a squib, "What ails the Republicans is too much oil, and what ails the Democrats is too much friction." He continued, "Take some of the Republican oil you have squeezed out of that party and put it on the wheels of the Democratic machine and ease up the friction."[25]

Adoo made him a tool of the Klan, and he was surprised and hurt when a number of fellow Catholics advised him that, as a Catholic, he had somehow forfeited all moral right to contest the nomination with another Catholic. One such plea came from a Boston school teacher:

> Since 1776 no Catholic has ever been nominated for President. Now, that there is some chance for a Catholic, for God's sake, don't you, another Catholic, stand in his way. Give him a clear road. Otherwise, it will be years again before another Catholic will have courage for such aspirations.[26]

A West Coast Democrat put the point more calmly, stressing Walsh's late start:

> Being a Roman Catholic a Democrat and of Irish parentage, I feel that I can speak quite candidly to you, . . .
>
> . . .
>
> Surely we, and every red-blooded Democrat are proud of you and your achievements, and had your name been brought out first, or before most of us became Smith-minded we should have all been for you. Then most likely the Klan Democrats would have opposed you.[27]

Walsh wrote the Boston schoolteacher that a candidate's religion was not "a proper consideration either for or against him. We shall occupy a very inconsistent position if we denounce those who oppose the candidate because of his religious beliefs or affiliations while we give him support upon any such ground."[28] He elaborated the theme in his reply to the West Coast Democrat:

> . . . I should hate to think that any of our co-religionists would think any the less of me because I choose to become a candidate for the nomination for president while Governor Smith is in

the race and the leading candidate. It would be distinctly displeasing to me to know that any one should support either him or me because we are Catholics. We have bitterly complained, and very justly complained that many people refused to vote for a candidate because he is a Catholic. How then shall we defend ourselves for supporting a man because he is a Catholic and how shall we justify our criticism of one Catholic because by his entrance into the race the chances of another Catholic may be minimized? I am not a candidate for the nomination because I am a Catholic. I hope to secure some support in the convention on the record I have made as a public official, because of the services I have rendered to the nation and the party and because of the policies and principles I in some degree represent.

. . .

There may be other reasons why I ought not to get into the race, but I can not admit for a moment that the fact that Governor Smith and I are both Catholics is any good reason, or any reason at all.[29]

The suggestion was often made that Walsh, a dry Catholic who was far removed from the Tammany Wigwam, would, if nominated, have carried the entire South. A case can be made for or against this view. Former Chief Justice C. S. Mann of Kentucky wrote early in 1929 that Walsh "would have carried every Southern State. . . ."* Walsh was not a completely objective witness, but here are the postelection thoughts of the Montana Senator on his probable fate in the South had he been accorded the nomination:

. . . Judge John Barton Payne who, . . . is a native of Virginia, told me in a quizzical way, that if all the people in Virginia

* Former Chief Justice Mann also wrote that Callahan ought to be elected Governor of Kentucky. It is often impossible to be sure where hope leaves off and analysis begins in the dispute about how well a dry Catholic would have fared at the polls.[30]

who said they would have voted for me had I been the nominee would actually have done so I would have carried that state by the biggest majority any candidate for the presidency ever received in it.

I am a little skeptical . . . that I would have been a popular candidate . . . in the South. You may recall that although it would seem that upon every consideration leaders in that section would have endeavored to promote the election of delegates to the national convention pledged to me, none of them did so.[31] *

In the twentieth century only Theodore Roosevelt, William Jennings Bryan, and, perhaps, Robert La Follette have captured the hearts of their followers as completely as did Al Smith. Certainly his host of urban backers would not have viewed tolerantly the substitution of Walsh to head the party ticket. The nomination of a Catholic would have enhanced the prestige of all Americans outside the dominant Protestant tradition, but there was far more to Smith, in the hearts of those who loved and shouted for him, than his religious affiliation. These personal as well as group associations were very important. Smith was loved and hated because he was a wet, a member of the Hall, a product of the East Side, and a Catholic. Particularly in the Northeast, where these associations were familiar, a feeling existed that if Smith failed of the nomination, the principal reason for it would be these associations and, chiefly,

* Against this judgment should be set the fact that Walsh had gone from high optimism to considerable pessimism in his reactions to the religious issue. Before his campaign foundered, Walsh made it clear that he would retain his faith in the essential fairness of the American people. But even before his primary defeat, the antics of the professional agitators, particularly those of his Senate colleague from Alabama, greatly distressed him.

his Catholicism. The nomination of Walsh, another Catholic, would not satisfy those who wanted Al Smith. From Maine came word:

> The sole issue with such members of our party in this part of the country as are Catholics is this in their minds,—will Al. Smith, known to all as being the greatest, most beloved, brilliant and ablest man in the party, the country, and I would say in the minds of most, the world, be deprived of the nomination because he is a Catholic and the K.K.K. control the Democratic party? It is no use to say that Walsh, too, is a Catholic.[32]

As convention time drew near it became increasingly improbable that either the drys or those opposed to running a Catholic had made any progress in their effort to block Smith's nomination. Confident that their candidate would be named at Houston, Smith's more astute political backers were more concerned about November. The bright sun of Republican prosperity was expected to melt the prospects of any Democratic candidate, though the incalculable factor of Smith's personal appeal made him the most promising of the Democrats. Yet to nominate a Catholic, however illustrious his record, would mark a milestone and strike a blow at prejudice.

Smith's nomination by the Houston convention was practically assured before the delegates arrived. The choice of him to head the ticket made it certain that the Catholic issue would have a large place in the campaign. It raised the broad issue whether the principle of religious freedom might be substantially jeopardized in the course of the campaign. Both Catholics and non-Catholics showed concern that so great a Constitutional right was in danger. Before Smith's nomination became practically certain, the unthinking had gone so far as to charge that Catholics in desperation were hatching some kind of plot.

Stanley Frost, the Washington journalist, insisted, on what evidence this writer has been unable to discover, that the idea of a separate political party was under serious consideration by leading Catholics. Michael Williams, editor of *Commonweal*, and William Bennett Munro, an outstanding political scientist, declared that any attempt to implement such an idea would be self-defeating. Williams was sure that responsible Catholics did not want a Catholic party in the United States, and unquestionably he was right.

There was real concern, however, because the first major party presidential nominee who was a Catholic appeared doomed to defeat. If he were to fail in November, there would be many whose resentment or frustration would not be assuaged by suggestions that prosperity and Prohibition accounted for the defeat.

There was genuine concern that the election of 1928 would validate in the eyes of many the contention that there was in fact an "unwritten law" that barred Catholics from the presidency. Catholics would have been less than normal if, after their great contributions to the national life, they had not resented a challenge to their eligibility to hold the highest elective office. This does not mean that there was in fact any likelihood of a Catholic political party. The advantages or disadvantages of forming such a party were discussed in several periodicals* and charges were made that leading Catholics were seriously weighing such political action. As Professor William Bennett Munro viewed it, however, Catholics had nothing to gain through a new party. In cities of heaviest Catholic concentration the creation of a Catholic party would, in Munro's opinion, have changed the existing Democratic party chiefly in nomenclature. He thought, too, that Catholics ought to have been satisfied with their not inconsiderable political triumphs. This view was sharply attacked by those Catholic leaders who freely acknowledged that their Church had fared well in the United States and who saw no reason for alarm in 1928 unless the so-called "unwritten law" should become the central and declared issue of the campaign. In fact, though the Catholic question was indeed a major one in 1928, it was not directly presented to the voter as a Constitutional issue. No campaign for the enactment of such an "unwritten law" could have succeeded, for the twenties in the United States were not Hitlerian in temper.

The two leading candidates for the Democratic nomination in 1928 were Catholic. One of them was nominated. This is a fact which should caution us against too sweeping an indictment of 1928 in the perspective of the long history of intolerance and bigotry. There was cause enough for shame, but the nomination

* The reader will find in the *Forum* and the *Christian Century* a coverage of the salient points: the conception of a deliverable Catholic vote and its implications, the lack of comparability between a hypothetical American Catholic party and Catholic parties in European countries, and the controversy over the amount of existing Catholic political influence in the United States.[33]

of one outside the dominant religious as well as social pattern was at least a modest advance. To this limited extent achievement in public life outweighed church affiliation.

An attitude such as anti-Catholicism was often so subtly blended as to be unrecognized by those possessed of it. Confusion was compounded in the not uncommon instances where anti-Catholic opinions were held by those who believed it reprehensible to be anti-Catholic. So, some who urged the nomination of Walsh in order to provide the means of demonstrating broad-mindedness betrayed inconsistencies in private expression. On such occasions, liquor, Tammany, and the Roman Catholic hierarchy were consigned conjointly, and with choice expletives, to an execrable place. Often the private letters supply proof of the existence of profound apprehensions and doubts on the part of educated Protestants about Catholicism. Despite Smith's public record and despite the remarkable manner in which he had publicly bared his soul as a Catholic and an American, the views of Charles Marshall were the convictions of great numbers of Americans. Probably the conviction that Marshall might be right was a more important source of political anti-Catholicism than all the noisy speeches of rabble-rousing Catholic-baiters such as Thomas J. Heflin.

The nomination of Governor Smith at Houston, Texas, was the result of many causes. His workers were energetic and not without hope that their candidate's personality would bring victory in November. Smith possessed a very rare quality of personal appeal. His reputation as Governor and geographical considerations were other key factors. One commentator noted that prior to Smith's nomination, Theodore Roosevelt represented the nearest approach to the nomination of a city man for President. But Roosevelt, typed as a rancher, was no part of the toiling city. Symbolically, the nomination of Al Smith in 1928 was as revolutionary as the choice of Jackson in 1828.[34] Though the sequel showed that the cosmopolitan urban voters were less well prepared to win the presidency in 1928 than the frontiersmen had been a century earlier, the fact that a real city man won the nomination was itself highly significant. It would have been significant had the nominee been a Protestant, but it befitted the complex of the modern metropolis that he should not belong to the religious tradition of rural and small-town America.

When the Democrats gathered at Houston, Smith had weathered many attacks, both as a wet and as a Catholic. Some party leaders who represented areas where his name was anathema realized that the Democracy had a bear by the tail and that something could be said for holding on. Many who had opposed Smith now regarded his nomination as inevitable and, if not desirable, as tolerable under the circumstances. His political stature was far above that of any Democrat since Wilson, and no one doubted his ability to inspire among many a great personal devotion.

In such unpropitious times even his Democratic opponents conceded that there might be some logic in riding out the bleak decade with the "Happy Warrior." There were many who idealized him and thought no one else could possibly win. There were at least a few who thought Smith ought not to be President, but who agreed that his devoted followers must have their day, for the sake of future party unity. There was a widespread belief that only by the nomination of their hero could Smith's followers be appeased. Defeat at Houston for so outstanding a spokesman of the newer American groups would mean that great numbers whose pride demanded recognition would feel rejected. To millions of Catholics, and to many non-Catholics, Smith's religion would be counted the reason for failure to nominate him.

Note on Knights of Columbus "Oath"

Perhaps the most widely circulated of all kinds of anti-Catholic propaganda was the spurious oath attributed to the Knights of Columbus. This "oath" appeared with each resurgence of anti-Catholicism. It was represented as the Fourth Degree Oath taken by members of the Catholic fraternal order. It appeared in various full and abbreviated forms. For example, there is in the Smith *Papers* a lurid advertisement of the Tom Watson Book Co. (Thomson, Ga.) for a book by its notoriously anti-Catholic owner, giving these extracts from the alleged oath:

> I declare and swear * * * that the pope is Christ's vice regent on earth * * * he hath power to destroy and disown allegiance to any Protestant ruler * * * or obedience to any of their laws * * * or officers. I shall * * * do my utmost to extirpate the heretical Protestant or Masonic doctrines and destroy their pretended powers * * * I will * * * wage war on Protestants and Masons * * * will spare neither, sex or condition * * * I will secretly use the poison cup * * * etc., etc. * * * Witness same with my name written with the point of this dagger dipped in my own blood * *

CHAPTER FIVE

A Campaign Within a Campaign

> "It is not that Governor Smith is a Catholic and a wet which makes him an offense to the villagers and town dwellers, . . . The whole Puritan civilization which has built a sturdy, orderly nation is threatened by Smith."[1]
>
> —William Allen White

Eastern sophisticates have referred frequently to parts of the South and West as the "Bible belt," a vaguely defined wasteland where shouting evangelists and "short-cut" clergymen held sway. The fight to preserve a Fundamentalist faith against the teaching of scientists who had rejected *Genesis* as the guide to creation had reached dramatic culmination at Dayton, Tennessee, where William Jennings Bryan and Clarence Darrow championed the opposing views.* Henry L. Mencken assigned Bryan's followers to the species *Boobus americanus.*[2] As it happened, they were in many

* Walter Lippmann's interpretation of the meaning of the 1925 Tennessee statute and the threat to prescribe the limits of freedom of teaching appears in his *American Inquisitors* (New York, 1928).

instances the same rural Americans who had been served so small a portion of the feast of the twenties. *Boobus americanus* was not too stupid to sense an urban attitude of condescension.

Above all it was New York City that symbolized the East to the depressed farmers and small-town Americans of Mencken's "Bible belt." To these the vast metropolis on the Hudson was a slum-crowded center of peoples whose derivation and habits excluded them from the vision of all that America had been founded to perpetuate. To many Americans, Al Smith's native city seemed more like Babylon than Main Street. To many in the South and West, Gotham was a dangerous and bewildering conglomeration of Jews and Catholics, with an admixture of some wrong-headed modernistic Protestants who drew their inspiration from Union Theological Seminary. To them New York's political organization was anathema. The city's social life, presided over by Texas Guinan, nightly defied the fundamentals of the Constitution. The city was impersonal and hard. Since 1924 southerners and westerners had often recalled the rude manners of Smith supporters in the galleries at Madison Square Garden. Dislike of New York had its provincial and ridiculous side, as typified by the warning from a McAdoo supporter in 1924 against yielding to such temptations as the chocolate dainties alleged to be part of the plot to break down resistance to the man who wore the Brown Derby.

It was easy to paint Smith as the personification of the worst features of the city. The Klan, which had spearheaded the attack on the Governor in 1923–1924,

This representation of Smith as the servant of the Catholic hierarchy appeared in The Fellowship Forum, *November 3, 1928. It is typical of the extreme anti-Catholic Klan propaganda. (New York State Library, Albany)*

again sounded its "Klarion Kall for a Krusade" to bar him from the White House. Many who did not join the Klan sympathized with this part of its program. Anti-Smith propaganda stressed the patriotic and moral duty to defeat the Catholic leader of the Repeal movement, the man whose ambition was decried as a terrible threat to the preservation of the racial, moral, and religious face of America. The cry to men and even more to women, was to prepare for battle. The forces of Evil were cunning and well organized. In 1928, unlike 1924, God-fearing Americans must try to save their country without a McAdoo to lead them.

The controversies over religion and the Eighteenth Amendment and the element of snobbery were principal ingredients in the social campaign of 1928. The liquor issue was near the top of the list. The Houston convention's nomination of dry, Methodist Senator Joseph T. Robinson of Arkansas for second place did not balance the Democratic ticket in the minds of those who championed Prohibition, who thought of Tammany as a uniquely wicked organization, and whose heritage included a deep substratum of hatred and fear of Roman Catholicism. Long before the convention met southerners had repeatedly warned that the South could not safely be counted upon to support Smith. His nomination would now put to the test the easy assurance of the editors of *The New York Times* that the South would remain ever faithful to the Democratic party.[3]

A hero to many and respected by many whose formal education had not obscured their power to discern political genius, Smith entered the campaign enormously handicapped. Prosperity and Republicanism were woven into a perfect garment. Prohibitionists were still politically dominant in great sections and the "Shadow of the Pope" frightened many voters. To win, despite all this, the Democrats had to assume the South would remain solid. Building on this supposedly immovable foundation, the New York Governor would have to win many electoral votes in the industrial belt from Maryland to Massachusetts. This would not be easy; but if Smith could not succeed, the chances for any other Democrat were indeed poor. Pondering the wisdom of nominating Smith, one should remember that some leaders who were not enthusiastically for him had supported his nomination because it seemed in the long run to make sense. The nomination of someone with less positive identifications perhaps would have made for a smoother, though listless, campaign, but the party had invested in Davis and decorum in 1924 with no positive results. The desire of all good Democrats was to forget 1924. There was an especially compelling logic in the nomination of Governor Smith in 1928. Not since Bryan and Theodore Roosevelt had there been such near-fanatical zeal for a presidential candidate. Smith, of course, had strong religious support, as well as opposition. He had powerful backing throughout much of urban America. This was not confined to the eastern cities. To slight his enthusiastic backers in 1928 might entail political risks that could easily outweigh the advantage of pleasing the South. To nominate and lose with Smith in 1928 might be the required price for keeping city Democrats within the party.

Smith's political assets were very considerable. There was widespread respect for his record as Governor of New York. This, together with his gift for attracting many by his intensely human personality, might produce the ground swell that would bring victory. The voters of the great urban centers saw in Al Smith the symbol of their own aspirations. He was their champion. Others who were personally lukewarm to the Governor believed that to ignore the "Happy Warrior" in 1928 would make a deep cleavage in the party. Some, to be sure, suggested that noisy pro-Smith Democrats had no possible haven outside their party, but the prevailing view among leaders was that appeasement of so important a group was political wisdom. It is clear that many would have explained a rejection of Smith at Houston as a defeat of a Catholic *qua* Catholic. The act of nominating a Catholic, however, was such a departure from precedent that it lessened the hurt and resentment that followed Smith's defeat in November.

Leaders of the eastern and dominant wing of the Democratic party, while willing to assume risks in the South in an effort to strengthen Smith's position in the Northeast, counted heavily upon the voting habits of southerners. Hindsight illumines the many warnings, made months and even years before Houston, that it was unsafe to assume that southerners, long used to being taken for granted and suffering from a galling sense of political impotence, would continue to play their historic role. The nomination of Smith, in defiance of majority southern opinion, was the chief of those frustrating events. After Houston perceptive politicians became vaguely aware that there was an unusual stirring among southern Democrats and that, narrowly conceived, history is not an infallible prophet.

A special grievance of all drys was Smith's wet telegram to the Houston convention after that body had nominated him. Pledging enforcement of the laws Smith left no doubt that he would advocate important changes. There must be no return to the "old evils that grew from the saloon, . . . a defunct institution . . . ," but Smith's telegram dramatically reasserted his conviction that "real temperance," rather than Prohibition, would be the means employed to end the "bootlegging and lawlessness . . . now prevalent throughout this country."[4] Smith's telegram made it impossible for the Democrats effectively to straddle the Prohibition issue. Southern and western dry Democrats could bolt, as a few did, but most supported Smith, advancing none too convincingly the argument that the Eighteenth Amendment and Prohibition enforcement would be safe as long as Congress remained politically dry. Carter Glass was sure "Governor Smith's great-grandchildren will be dead and forgotten . . ."[5] before Congress would adopt and the states approve a repeal amendment.

The nomination of Smith, in conjunction with his telegram to the convention, gave the Republicans a monopoly on the use of the carefully worded phrase which characterized the Eighteenth Amendment as "noble in purpose." Dry Democrats were distressed by Smith's nomination; his wet telegram to the convention after that body had adopted a moderate plank on Prohibition provoked explosive anger among the more ardent

Prohibitionists. It was the last straw. The tide of anti-Smith sentiment was unleashed. Writing to McAdoo, George Fort Milton revealed this mood:

This unbroken series of events all indicates clearly to me that the Smith decision is to make the most brazn [*sic*] and frantic attempt possible to win the east; to do so with an appeal so wet that whiskey is dry by comparison. Such an appeal would have collateral aspects. It would be primarily to appetite, and secondarily to every sort of group complex, inferiority attitude, and resentment to American standards and ideals which could be contrived. To the aliens, who feel that the older America, the America of the Anglo-Saxon stock, is a hateful thing which must be overturned and humiliated; to the northern negroes, who lust for social equality and racial dominance; to the Catholics who have been made to believe that they are entitled to the White House, and to the Jews who likewise are to be instilled with the feeling that this is the time for God's chosen people to chastise America yesteryear.

. . . If the dominance of such groups represent the new America which Smith is seeking to arouse, the Old America, the America of Jackson, and of Lincoln and Wilson, should rise up in wrath and defeat it.

. . .

. . . As great as have been my doubts about Hoover, he is sprung from American soil and stock; . . . [6]

Nothing that was to occur during the campaign would change the fact that such an approach to Smith's candidacy portended no good for his cause in states where farm and small-town people were predominant.

In the Northeast precampaign prospects offered more hope for Smith, but there was no real assurance. Few among the political prophets would predict victory for the Governor without starting with the assumption that his home state would support him. But betting, favorable to Smith at one time, changed to even odds that Hoover would carry New York. This perforce meant that many New Yorkers who had repeatedly supported Smith for governor would oppose him for the presidency. An unprecedentedly large up-state Republican vote seemed likely to offset the expected big Al Smith vote in the city.

One of the explanations for Smith's relative lack of strength in New York in 1928 helps account for his problems in other states as well. Doubts were voiced about the breadth of his knowledge of national affairs. Liabilities, of course, are relative; this one was the more serious because of the other felt deficiencies of the Democratic candidate. The presidency was thought to be an office so great as to raise the stature of an average politician from Ohio or Vermont, endowing breadth of vision and world-mindedness on a Harding or a Coolidge but not on a product of New York's East Side. Smith's career had been a notable demonstration of growth in statesmanship, but he could better have advanced his cause as a presidential aspirant had he made a more serious effort to nationalize himself. The cost would not have been great. An example of a missed opportunity was the Governor's refusal to heed the urgings of friends who wished him to share the publicity which benefitted Secretary of Commerce Hoover in connection with aid to Mississippi flood victims in 1927. It is doubtful, however, whether the so-called evidence in support of the view that Smith lacked an understanding of the national problems would have seriously hurt him had this been an isolated objection. By all reasonable tests Smith had proved his capacity for growth. His great talent in the art of government was widely acknowledged by outstanding men in both parties, and his excellent record as Governor was admitted by most discerning and fair-minded men.*

Some of the eastern elite and many in the South and West were convinced that Smith was not socially acceptable. As early as 1924 suggestions had been made that someone with the background and education of Franklin D. Roosevelt would meet all the social requirements. The irony is interesting—Smith, the socially rejected, was never a radical and made considerable gestures in the direction of conservatism in 1928. The reader may ponder the sequel in the thirties when Smith, the Liberty Leaguer, joined the unpopular movement against Roosevelt, the "traitor to his class." There is much evidence in the letters of the campaign months that many educated Americans, as well as others quite incapable of phrasing their thoughts grammatically, regarded Al Smith as much below the presidential standard in educational and social background. Smith's background made him utterly unacceptable to those who looked upon him with condescension as well as those who considered a formal education a necessary prerequisite for the presidency.

He suffered, too, because of his affiliation with an organization regarded over much of the land as uniquely iniquitous, Tammany Hall. The reputation of Tammany was, indeed, a very important part of the campaign. To a degree the loud protests against the Hall

* No serious study has yet been made of Smith's governorship.

were ill-defined emotional outcries. Like other city machines, Tammany had its notorious past and questionable present, but it would never do in 1928 to admit that Croker and Tweed were dead. Well-known journalists and clergymen vied with one another in denouncing the Tiger. Relatively few voters understood that Smith had long since emerged from the position of a servant of the Hall. The contemporary anti-Tammany book by Morris R. Werner became a part of the anti-Smith propaganda.[7]

All too often it has been represented that the several phases of the "social campaign" were essentially camouflage for the real issue, anti-Catholicism. This is a great oversimplification. The enforcement of Prohibition, the problem of immigration, and snobbery were among the social issues that were profoundly important to the American people. These issues and the issue of religion were often so badly confused that an effort to isolate them does violence to their interrelated complexity. Prohibition, especially, was often made to play hide-and-seek with the religious issue, the game often becoming so obfuscated that there was constant argument about which was which. From July to November the air was rent with charges and recriminations that religious bigotry hid beneath the reputable issue of ending the tyranny of booze by adherence to the Eighteenth Amendment.

There can be no doubt that the enforcement, by statute, of the ban on alcoholic beverages was an issue of great importance in its own right; probably no specific social issue in the campaign was more important. Each party was pledged to uphold the Amendment, though, as we have seen, Governor Smith's telegram to the Houston convention, together with his known opposition to the Amendment, put Democratic drys in a most uncomfortable position. The difficulty was great because most, though not all, Prohibition advocates were wholeheartedly dedicated to the cause. As in the eighteen fifties when abolition was to some *the* reform, so now millions were so fully committed to Prohibition that there was no place in their hearts for any other reform, temperance included. Strong support came from many business leaders. In an era of industrial boom Henry Ford voiced the conviction of much of the business community that the Eighteenth Amendment was essential for prosperity.

To thousands of the clergy and to millions of the lay members of the evangelical churches Prohibition was to all practical purposes an article of faith. References to seeming Biblical support for temperance, rather than prohibition, were overlooked; constructive arguments using Holy Writ did not in this instance stress textual literalism even though the arguments were often made by Fundamentalists. Knowing full well the tragic social evils attendant on drunkenness, these good and sincere people, politically powerful in the rural West and dominant in the South, had no faith in temperance. Warnings against statutory prohibition by those who greatly feared that lawlessness threatened the foundations of government were tossed aside as evidence of an evil desire to nullify the Constitution and of a shameful disregard of religion and morality.

Widespread urban prosperity more than any other reason explains why most political prognosticators were confident the voters would not remove the Republicans from power in 1928. The real and prolonged distress among the nation's farmers appeared to offer partially offsetting political advantages to the opposition, but the controlling eastern wing of the Democratic party failed to capitalize on the opportunity. In fact, Smith had not fully studied the farm problem. He was less than surefooted in handling the controversial equalization fee. The task of convincing distressed farmers that Smith understood their problems was not an easy one. Cartoonists had a field day with the "Tammany Farmer." The New York *Herald Tribune*[8] showed Smith, encased in a beer barrel, smiling ingratiatingly at a young animal labelled "Farm Vote." In the background is a creature called Tammany instructing "Al" to "make a noise like farm aid."* The picture of the New Yorker, in brown derby and gay tie, peering over a farm fence, half defeated in advance any farm program Democratic brain trusters could devise.

The problems before us in this book relate but indirectly to the economic issues of the campaign. The special conditions of the temper of the twenties suggest that the prosperity-depends-on-continued-Republican-rule argument was almost certainly the principal reason for Smith's failure to keep pace with Hoover. But the record vote for both candidates can hardly be explained

* Anti-Smith forces evidently cherished this effort for it appeared on the cover of a pamphlet found in the Smith *Papers*.

without an understanding of the untypical and emotion-packed social issues. With the Democracy conservative both in platform and campaign management, the traditional preference of business for the Republicans provides less than a full explanation for the extraordinary size of the total vote.*

The pains taken by the Democrats to win the confidence of business, not only by platform conservatism but by various other devices, is understandable. Since the party had traded Cleveland for Bryan, it had largely failed to win the confidence of the business community. To alter this condition greatly in a decade when the "business of America was business" and when the Republicans enjoyed a sort of marital relationship with prosperity proved impossible. Though the Democratic

* In the election Hoover defeated Smith by an electoral vote of 444 to 87. The more meaningful popular vote figures are less startling when it is recalled that just under 400,000 (1.08 per cent) votes cast for President in 1928 went to candidates other than Smith or Hoover, whereas the third party candidate in 1924, Robert M. La Follette, polled nearly five million (17.13 per cent) votes. Yet the 1928 story is remarkable enough: (1) the total vote for President was greater—by almost eight million—than in 1924; (2) Smith's vote exceeded Davis' 1924 vote by over six and one-half million (Hoover's was five and one-half million over Coolidge's); (3) the total vote for President in 1932 was less than three million more than the 1928 vote, whereas the candidates and issues of 1928 brought out nearly seven and three-quarters million more than voted for Coolidge, Davis, and La Follette in 1924.

As usual the county vote is most illuminating. In 1928, 2,080 counties reported more votes for Smith than Davis received in 1924; in 997 counties there was a drop. The immense Hoover strength is revealed in the fact that his vote exceeded Coolidge's 1924 vote in over 95 per cent of the counties. See Edgar Eugene Robinson, *The Presidential Vote 1896-1932* (Palo Alto, 1934), 21-27, 402.

platform contained little if anything to alarm business, in the course of the campaign Republicans insisted that some of Smith's statements showed a leaning toward experimentation and were therefore, if not socialistic, at least dangerous to the unruffled calm presided over by Coolidge. True, a substantial number of important business and financial leaders backed Smith, but their number fell far short of changing the conviction that the Republican party was the guarantor of the upward business spiral.

Smith's most dramatic move to win business support was the appointment of John J. Raskob Chairman of the Democratic National Committee. Raskob was a Catholic, a militant member of the National Association Against Prohibition, a New Yorker, and a member of the Union League Club which was opened only to Republicans. He had reportedly voted for Coolidge. On the face of it, this appointment seemed like an insult to the dry, Protestant, rural South. But Raskob was Vice President and Chairman of the Finance Committee of one of America's biggest industries, General Motors. He was so great a financial genius and spokesman for big business that the stock market boomed when he opined optimistically on the state of General Motors,[9] and again when he assured the country, from Houston:

> Alfred E. Smith, as President would give the country a constructive business Administration. Business, big or little, has nothing to fear from Governor Smith. There is no occasion for business timidity during a Presidential campaign. Business has outgrown the feeling that there is something to fear in campaign years. It is on too big a scale for that.[10]

This statement caused such a flurry of buying that on Wall Street it was called a "Smith Market." It is no wonder that some of Smith's political advisers were willing to take this gamble with Smith's personal friend. Raskob's rise to wealth was in the Horatio Alger tradition. Of Alsatian stock, his father a cigarmaker, Raskob was born in New York State. As a very young man he started at $7.50 a week, supporting his mother and a brother and two sisters. He then got a job as stenographer in the employ of Pierre S. du Pont. In an incredibly short time he rose to Vice President in charge of finance for the E. I. du Pont de Nemours Company. By his mid-thirties he and du Pont had gained voting control of General Motors. Calm and efficient, with a "driving force derived from optimism . . ." Raskob had proved his wizardry at making much out of little. He is said to have made into millionaires eighty General Motors executives whom he persuaded to invest in their own company. Some of those who joined the charmed circle did so after only four years and an original investment of $25,000.[11] Governor Smith had appointed a man of considerable business acumen.

Some Democratic leaders favored the Raskob appointment, but from the first many were dissatisfied. Writing to Josephus Daniels, Franklin D. Roosevelt expressed a vague feeling of apprehension. Roosevelt, who had been introduced to Raskob only the day before Smith made him National Chairman, described the appointment as a "bold stroke to try to end the 99% of business (big and little) preference for the Republican Party." Realizing perhaps better than Smith how the

The Democratic candidate of 1928 and his National Chairman, John J. Raskob, on the porch of the Raskob home at Claymount, Delaware, October 28, 1928. (Brown Brothers, New York, N. Y.)

appointment would be received by hard-pressed southern Democratic leaders, Roosevelt wrote that Democratic success was impossible without "the big industrial states." But the future President was unhappy.

Frankly, I am more and more disgusted and bored with the thought that in this great nation, the principal issue may be drawn into what we do or do not put into our stomachs. Are there no great fundamentals of the science and practice of government left?[12]

Raskob had intended, according to first reports, to retain his two positions, Chairman of the Democratic National Committee and of the Finance Board of General Motors. In fact, he located the Democratic National headquarters in the building that housed the General Motors offices, the better to carry on both his jobs. However, he soon resigned his duties with General Motors. There was speculation that the Board of General Motors had put pressure on him to do so. There was an air of forced optimism in the Smith camp, despite the disappointment that the Raskob appointment had failed to rally top industrial leaders to Smith's side.[13]

Raskob's religion remained to plague him throughout the campaign. Had Smith been a Protestant, Raskob's Catholicism would not have been political dynamite. Unlike the Catholicism of Thomas J. Walsh, Raskob's religious affiliation was conspicuous. He had recently made very large gifts to Catholic agencies for which he had been thanked personally in an audience with Pius XI.[14] It is no wonder that Raskob proved incapable from the start of making a positive contribution to easing the pressures that threatened to explode the foundations of the Democracy in the South.

Before Labor Day the candidates delivered their acceptance speeches, reserving their major addresses for September and October. During July and August Republicans daily re-emphasized their delicate relationship to prosperity. Democrats played up news of the defections of any business leaders. Many of these were little known or were men avowedly opposed to the Eighteenth Amendment. The formal campaign marked time until autumn.

A perceptive voter with memories of past campaigns needed no reminder, as he read his July newspapers, that this campaign had special aspects that distinguished it sharply from other political contests. The nomination of Smith made this inescapable. It was no novelty to run a New York Governor for president; it was unprecedented to run one who had risen from the East Side. A corollary of this is that it soon became clear that this campaign acquired its unusual character less from what the Democratic candidate would say than from his total background and associations, real and fancied. Small-town Americans, their minds filled with *ex parte* reports of what Governor Smith was like, generally agreed with the famed journalistic exponent of the older America, William Allen White, that the bid of this new spokesman of the eastern cities must be defeated. The campaign to defeat Smith early assumed a character which cannot be recalled without shame.

There was considerable quibbling during the campaign about the proper descriptive term for the morally slanderous attacks on Smith. When the campaign was described as one of whispering it was pointed out, with technical accuracy, that there was plenty of denunciation of Smith in tones easily heard across large auditoriums. That argument lacks any moral meaning; the social campaign to defeat Alfred E. Smith was, much of it, a whispering campaign. Circumstantial and some direct evidence substantiates the point that many of the shouted denunciations of the Democratic candidate had their origin in whispered innuendoes. A sample of these was the widely circulated story that Smith was commonly drunk on speaking occasions. Let Governor Smith recount what happened.

. . . Suddenly, as though by a pre-concerted arrangement a story started to circulate about me, and came from various parts of the country with the same general purport. A woman in Syracuse wrote to a woman in West Virginia that I was intoxicated at the New York State Fair on Governor's Day and to such a degree that it required two men to hold me up while I was delivering an address from the grandstand. A Republican state senator who acted as escort to me that day by appointment from the State Department of Agriculture, flatly denied that any such thing happened. Photographs and motion pictures had been taken of me from the minute I entered the fair grounds until I stepped aboard the New York Central train to go home. These showed plainly that the story had absolutely no foundation in fact. When the lie was nailed the woman in West Virginia refused to produce the letter and the woman in Syracuse denied that she had written it.

Shortly after that a Protestant minister from Albany in the course of a speech delivered at a Chautauqua in Indiana made the statement that I was so intoxicated while talking over the radio on the Sunday my family returned from Texas that it required two men to hold me up. When I sent for him he denied that he had ever made any such statement, although the Democratic National Committee was in possession of six different affidavits from six reputable people stating that they had heard him say it.

The whispering campaign along these lines evidently had its origin in some one place because half a dozen different stories were carried back to me and each time my supposed degree of intoxication was so great that it required two men to hold me up.

... Whenever I went anywhere I was always accompanied by two people and generally one on each side of me. One was my bodyguard and the other person someone supposed to escort me to the place where I was going to speak. I seldom walked alone. It was this that enabled them to get away with the story that two people had to hold me up.[15]

Some of the slander in this unofficial campaign was directed against Herbert Hoover, but it is a mistake to suppose that the Republican candidate suffered personal abuse in a way remotely comparable to that heaped on Smith. Mr. Hoover, in his *Memoirs*, has expressed the view that the two slander campaigns canceled out.[16] The weight of evidence does not support this view. Much of the slander against Smith was of ancient vintage. The aim was to persuade voters that the man who had been repeatedly re-elected New York's Governor was "rum soaked"; often the charge was compounded to make him a "rum soaked Romanist." We have here another example of the fact that a clear separation of the prohibition and religious issues is impossible. Circumstantial evidence points to the common origin of many of the anti-Smith stories. An example is the portion of the slander campaign aided and abetted by William Allen White and, later, by the Reverend John Roach

Straton. White's character makes his participation in the low-level campaign the more significant.

It appears that the Superintendent of the New York Civic League, the Reverend O. R. Miller of Albany, had furnished every newspaper publisher in the United States with a copy of a circular, first published and distributed by the Anti-Saloon League in 1918, that purported to be a summary of Governor Smith's record in the New York legislature between 1904 and 1916. The principal allegation against Smith was that his legislative record showed that he favored prostitution as well as the saloon. These allegations reached the Kansas editor, William Allen White. What White did with them is an amazing exhibit in the 1928 slander campaign.

This was not the first instance of White's interest in Governor Smith. Two years earlier he had authored a popular article in *Collier's Weekly* in which he dubbed Smith "a dresser" with "pink-and-crimson tie" who "took orders from Tammany until he was able to give orders." The 1924 convention, wrote the Emporia novelist and journalist, "was between the hard, ascetic moralities of Puritanism and the lighter, brighter, happier philosophy of Catholicism. . . ." White thought Smith had the capacity for national leadership "if he will take it," but judged it might take a decade to educate the New York Governor to the point where he could know his country sufficiently to exercise the duties of the presidency. The Kansan was convinced that there was "no stronger brain in America than Smith's."[17] There was a measure of high praise in this portrait done in 1926. The confused and distressing nature of White's 1928 attack was heightened by the fact that in his forthcoming book, *Masks in a Pageant*, he was about to present Smith in an essentially favorable light. As the New York *Herald Tribune* said:

> "All the politics," Mr. White will say in the book, "that Al Smith learned of the old order under Tom Foley was a capacity for teamwork, a habit of industry and the precious moral precept that it does not pay to lie.
>
> "Much may be said for the Croker kind of politics. It did make square men who, according to the morals of their day, played a fair, brave game, even when it was dirty. When the morals changed, the habits of the game did not . . . it was as square as the game that Lincoln learned or Jackson."[18]

In the light of the foregoing, and because William Allen White represented progress and honesty in public life and was as good an image of midwest America as could be found, his role in the slander campaign against Smith becomes doubly significant and unusually eloquent of the depth and spread of the campaign of vilification and misrepresentation.

The day after the Raskob appointment, White attacked the Democratic nominee in a speech before the Kansas Republican convention. He charged that Smith's votes in the New York Assembly proved not only that the Democratic candidate was the friend of the saloon but also that he had been politically allied with organized vice, including prostitution. Reviewing Smith's legislative record, White said Smith

> . . . had voted ten times against allowing the people to vote on any sort of a restriction on the sale of liquor; four times against stopping gambling and prostitution in connection with saloons; three times against repealing the law keeping saloons

open on Sunday; four times in favor of removing zoning restrictions which would keep open saloons from churches and schools and three times in favor of laws sponsored by organized gambling.[19]

Along with his friendly-to-vice charges White coupled a tribute to Smith as a man of "unusual intelligence, splendid courage and rare political wisdom . . ."! Aside from the charges about prostitution and vice, White's speech was mainly a typical attack on Tammany. He denounced the Hall, charging that Smith's record showed slavish obedience to that organization. He saw the coming election as a struggle between two concepts of life. The contest, he believed, was for the future of America. He insisted that small-town America's opposition to Smith was due neither to his religion nor to his views on Prohibition:

> It is not that Governor Smith is a Catholic and a wet which makes him an offense to the villagers and town dwellers, but because his record shows the kind of President he would make —a Tammany President.
>
> . . .
>
> Tammany is Tammany, and Smith is its prophet, . . . The whole Puritan civilization which has built a sturdy, orderly nation is threatened by Smith.[20]

Of course one important facet of the "whole Puritan civilization" was its stanchly Protestant character. The Eighteenth Amendment was also now commonly regarded as part of that civilization. Governor Smith was frequently quoted as having said in 1923 that he hoped for the day when "we could put our foot on the rail and blow off the froth." Would not his election, whatever he had said in 1923 or later, impair the Eighteenth Amendment? White warned that there were "... learned and respectable famous lawyers ... [who] believe that the Eighteenth Amendment is unconstitutional"[21] and that Smith as President, could be counted upon to appoint them to the Supreme Court. This was an answer to those hard pressed southern drys who contended that Smith as President could do nothing to endanger Prohibition.

It is not surprising to find that Smith was outraged by what he, along with those who had followed his career closely, knew to be a slander, the charge that he had been on the side of organized vice. Sure that White's "facts" could be traced to the Reverend O. R. Miller, Smith denounced the Albany clergyman as "an eighteen-carat professional faker." It was not necessary for Smith to argue this point before a New York press corps; but, as one of the reporters remarked, the Reverend Miller was "a bigger man in Kansas" than in the state of New York.[22] Much of the United States was Kansas writ large. As for the Sage of Emporia, Governor Smith did not mince words. He charged complete misrepresentation.

The extreme seriousness of White's charge against Smith stirred up a hornets' nest. The famed Emporia editor was not really alone in this enterprise. He enlisted the financial aid of the Republican National Committee.[23] Two "experts" spent a fortnight examining Smith's Albany votes. They gave White the "complete record" and at least a temporary sense of confidence. In a New York press interview White continued his dubious approach by praising Smith's intelligence and courage while denouncing his alleged subservience to Tammany Hall and his imputed reprehensible past. White declared:

> No Klansman in a boob legislature, . . . cringing before a kleagle or a wizard, was more subservient to the crack of the whip than was Al Smith—ambitious and effective and smart as chain lightning—in the Legislature when it came to a vote to protect the saloon, to shield the tout and to help the scarlet woman of Babylon, whose tolls in those days always clinked regularly in the Tammany till.
>
> . . .
>
> . . . I make no claim here that Smith is a Tammany plug-ugly. I honor him for having risen from the debasing subserviency of those who in the days of his youth sweated dimes from the poor through those who prey on the poor—the saloon-keeper, the tout and the prostitute. This record is, of course, an old record of a young man. But the young man rose on this record. And to-day the issue is formed upon the elements that made this old record—the return of the saloon which Governor Smith as a young man defended so ably, so consistently, so loyally. But the Tammany system goes on to-day, as it went on 100 years ago, and, indeed, as it will go on in our American cities unless Governor Smith and the sinister forces behind him are overthrown. Tammany is indeed Tammany, and Smith is its Major Prophet.[24]

On July 30 White again pressed the attack, offering to furnish photostatic records of Smith's Assembly votes.[25] Much of this concerned saloon legislation, but quite naturally it was the charge that Smith had voted in the interests of the oldest profession that attracted most attention. Immediately after his detailed attack on Smith, White talked with his friend Walter Lippmann. Lippmann explained to White that ". . . Smith had voted against bills to regulate gambling and prostitution because he had felt that these laws were unconstitutional, unenforceable, and that they would encourage police corruption."[26]

Whatever the cause, the Kansan decided after a sleepless, conscience stricken night that he had "hit below the belt" and retracted his charge that Smith had been subservient to organized vice. Smith was thus unburdened of the onus of favoring prostitution and gambling. "It was a case of conscience," winning out later on, said White, who added that the prostitution charge had been made "without thinking deeply about it."[27] He even managed to have the vice charges deleted from some later editions of the New York papers. When last interviewed before embarking on his trip abroad, he said his one end in view was "to purge myself of all my sins."[28]

Democratic newspapers now claimed White had made a retraction and that Smith's record was cleared. Apparently this development had been foreseen both by White and by at least one prominent figure high in the Republican party councils. On August 15, through the Republican National Committee Publicity Chairman, Henry J. Allen, a statement by White was released as a "cable" from Paris. White had left the letter with Allen before going to Europe, and Allen released it as a Paris cable "to increase its effectiveness."[29] White said he had made no retractions but had only amended his charges: "On the prostitution issue I proved my case," the editor cabled, "got a conviction and suspended the sentence. I only did this because I felt that a debate on the subject of harlotry was not worthy of a Presidential campaign."[30]

The retraction of August 1 had not been altogether forthright. White's "cable" from Paris made an already gauche situation more ridiculous. With each new statement White dug himself more deeply in the mire. In a letter to *The New York Times*, Elmer Davis stated the case with brevity and acid truth: "There ought to be some Pulitzer prize to give adequate recognition to the unique talent of William Allen White. None of the rest of us can put so much poison into a libel as he manages to leave in a retraction."[31]

White's praise-and-damnation assault on Smith was not made as an attack on the Governor's religion, but it was characteristic of the whispering campaign that these and similar vice charges were often used as supporting props by anti-Catholic propagandists. The longer the list of Smith's allegedly evil associations, the more dangerous each, including his Romanism, appeared to those whose minds were preconditioned to believe the worst.

Smith's reply to White was delayed until August 20. This seems to have been the result of an understandable perplexity among his advisers on how attacks of this sort should be met without worsening a bad situation. Smith's decision to risk the great political danger of assuming the defensive appears to have been based on the belief that through a reply to White, a man of national stature, he might come to grips with the whole battery of charges that centered about his Tammany background. White's charges offered an opportunity comparable to that afforded by Marshall's challenge to his religion fifteen months earlier. It was felt that, in answering White, it might be possible to put a curb on the entire smear campaign. An optimistic pro-Smith journalist, Charles Willis Thompson, later wrote of White's charges:

> Smith was waiting for just that. He was waiting as he had waited when the whispering campaign about the Vatican ruling the United States was running along the hedges; waiting until Charles C. Marshall, a man good enough for his notice, voiced it, and then smashed it in the solar plexus. This subterranean slander about whiskey and prostitution could not be met while it was voiced only by sewer rats. White was the man Smith was waiting for. . . .[32]

Of course, the tragedy of Smith's situation was the fact that it was only too easy to do serious damage through accusation alone.

Before Smith had decided whether or how best to answer White, the Kansan's charges were seized upon, embroidered, and again hoisted high for public view by a prominent New York City minister. The Reverend Doctor John Roach Straton was a veteran battler for revealed religion and moral truth as defined by John Roach Straton. A decade earlier he had left a Virginia pulpit for the greater forum of New York City's Calvary Baptist Church. He enjoyed also the wider audience provided by radio station WQAO. He was a leader of the nation-wide Fundamentalist movement and was in constant conflict with all aspects of urban wickedness, including ". . . card playing, cocktail drinking, poodle dogs, divorce, novels, stuffy rooms, dancing, evolution, Clarence Darrow, overeating, nude art, prize-fighting, actors, greyhound racing and modernism."[33]

Dr. Straton sensed in Governor Smith's nomination a new and immediate mission, one sufficiently urgent to justify the temporary abandonment of his attacks on his habitual enemies. On August 5 Straton opened fire in a Sunday evening service. The subject of his sermon was "The Moral and Religious Stakes in the Present Political Situation—A Frank Discussion of the Dangers of Electing as President of the United States Any Man Who Advocates the Nullification of Righteous Law, and Whose Election Would Inevitably Give Aid and Comfort to the Forces of Lawlessness, Immorality, Vice and Crime in America."[34] Like the sermon titles of colonial divines it was itself a barrage. In reviving and reiterating White's gambling and prostitution charges, Dr. Straton picked up where White had left off. Straton was sure that the Kansan's withdrawal of his vice charges against Smith was actuated merely by "the charity of a noble heart." But Straton said that these charges remained a part of Smith's record and that the Democratic candidate was "the deadliest foe in America to-day of the forces of moral progress and true political wisdom."[35]

Smith was indignant at what he quite naturally regarded as an attack on his character. In a letter to Straton, Smith demanded the opportunity to answer the charges in the place where they had been made, Calvary Baptist Church. He expressed an unwillingness to impute unworthy motives to Straton for his attack, since it was "made in a church devoted to the teachings of Christ, one of which was 'Thou shalt not bear false witness against thy neighbor.' "[36] The reporters reached Straton before he received Smith's letter. When informed of the letter's contents, the clergyman accepted the Governor's challenge but suggested Madison Square Garden as more suitable than Calvary Church. (At a later time Straton's assistant thought Yankee Stadium would be the proper place.) As though to prove that he had not forgotten his old enemies, Straton volunteered that the fight to keep Smith out of the White House was part of his old struggle with the evolutionists, since "the teaching of evolution and materialism is responsible for law nullification. . . ." Though it was scarcely possible to brand Smith an evolutionist, Wickedness, like Truth, was indivisible. The Protestant clergyman said that he would not bring the Catholic religion into the debate. "I do not see that it will be necessary." He was not sure that religion could be kept out of the campaign in the South. The Doctor, as it happened, was already planning a tour of the South and made a taunting challenge to Smith to make it a joint junket.[37]

In accepting Governor Smith's challenge, and in calling for Madison Square Garden as the place for the debate, Straton asked:

> . . . a division of seating—say, to the number of 3,000 for our Calvary members and my friends and the same number, say, to St. Patrick's Cathedral congregation and your friends, the other 20,000 seats to be equally divided between the Democratic and Republican headquarters for distribution.[38]

This drawing by Rollin Kirby in the New York World *typifies the violent feeling against Smith displayed by some Protestant clergymen. The cartoonist's caption was: "Though I speak with the tongues of men and angels, and have not charity, I am become as sounding brass, or a tinkling cymbal. 1 Corinthians XIII - 1." (Museum of the City of New York)*

Straton then instructed the Governor, whom he asked to remember that he was not yet President, on the correct use of the Bible. He advised Smith that the injunction against bearing "false witness," which Smith had quoted in his letter to Straton, was not Christ's teaching but came from the Old Testament. Christ, he said, had superseded the Old Testament with the "law of love." Straton said he had followed the teachings of the New Testament in his attack on Smith; he had spoken "in love." He reminded Smith also that when the Scriptures declared that "the powers that be (the Constitution of the United States) are ordained of God," the Eighteenth Amendment is clearly included under "powers."[39]

Straton's trustees' objection to a debate with Smith in Calvary Church posed a problem for Straton. Nothing abashed, the clergyman simply stepped up his onslaughts. On Sunday evening, August 12, Straton's son read to the congregation a statement by his father. It contained a number of interesting points. The debate, said Straton, must take place somewhere. As for the religious issue, the clergyman insisted that his indictment of Smith was no different in kind from that of "some of our Catholic friends" when they denounced Senator Heflin. And in making his vice charges against Smith, Straton suggested that he had acted merely as Christ had done when he used the "whip of small cords" against the "corruptionists of the time."[40]

Smith now demanded a yes or no answer on the use of Calvary Church. Fair play, he said, dictated that the reply must be made in the place where Straton had voiced his charges.[41] Straton, unable to comply, was full of new plans to have the grand debate in New York City followed by a sort of Lincoln-Douglas tour of the South. With the prospects of any debate dwindling rapidly, Straton conjured up an elaborate procedure which provided rejoinders, a "surrebuttal" for Smith if the Governor wished one, and an equal division of time, reserving, however, for the Reverend Doctor Straton the privilege "to close the meeting with prayer. . . ."[42] And so, with Straton grandiloquently flourishing the language of the code duello before Smith and the newspaper public, the subject disappeared as an item of top news. In a final blast, the Fundamentalist leader assured Smith that he would certainly meet him:

> Unless you stand up to your own challenge, your action in running to cover will leave me free to take whatever steps in the matter I may deem wise and proper and will AUTOMATICALLY BRAND YOU BEFORE THE WORLD AS A BLUFFER, A TAMMANY TRICKSTER AND A COWARD.[43]

The debate never took place.

The New York *Herald Tribune* quite properly handled the Straton story as low melodrama. But this pro-Hoover paper refrained from direct editorial comment on it until the pro-Smith New York *World* had made *l'affaire Straton* the occasion for heaping more praise on Smith. The *World* characterized the 1928 campaign as one of poisonous whispering against the Democratic candidate. To this the *Herald Tribune* made the rejoinder that Straton's pulpit voice was audible over considerable distances. The *World* insisted that the whispered stories about Smith and the outpourings of the

Stratons over the land were made from the same propaganda cloth. Referring to the slanderous stories that were now in wide circulation, the *Herald Tribune* in an editorial, quoted the *World* as expressing its certainty that "Mr. Hoover will not repeat them, of course. We feel certain that he is too much of a gentleman not to feel extremely uncomfortable at being the beneficiary of these slanders." The *Herald Tribune* countered that in this very statement the *World* had furnished a good example of the ingredients of a "whispering campaign":

This innuendo, giving the impression that Herbert Hoover really benefits by slanders circulated against Governor Smith, is as absurd an exaggeration as the rest of "The World's" tub thumping. Herbert Hoover's appeal is a positive appeal, resting securely on the nation-wide confidence which he has inspired in his ability to solve the country's problems. It has never been suggested before that he depended on slanderous whisperings about Governor Smith for his success at the polls; and, solely on grounds of good taste, it is to be hoped that this suggestion will not be made again.

The plain fact is, that in challenging Dr. Straton, Governor Smith acknowledged the fact that the bitterest fight in this campaign is inside his own party. Dr. Straton's mentality is typical of a certain bigotry which prevails in the Democratic South. In giving battle to him, Governor Smith is really battling with his fellow Democrats. Republicans will merely stand by as onlookers while Dr. Straton and Governor Smith whisper their debate over the radio.[44]

Had Smith been prudent in seizing the gauntlet laid down by the sensational Dr. Straton who had insisted that the Democrats, when they nominated Smith, had made "a covenant with death" and "were in agreement with hell"?[45] There had been divisions among his own advisers, the majority counseling action. The case for taking cognizance of Dr. Straton was probably based on the Governor's known ability in debate. The fact is that it was Smith's entry into this affair that catapulted Straton's charges from deep inside the newspapers to page one.

Straton pursued Smith long after Smith had dropped this unfortunate affair. The clergyman told his congregation of the terrible dangers ahead if Al Smith ever reached the White House. But at one point he brought good tidings to his congregation. The divine decision on the forthcoming election had been revealed to Dr. Straton by a supernatural sign. It had come at a moment of great mental depression which had reached its nadir on the eve of the Smith notification ceremonies at Albany, when the candidate was scheduled to deliver his acceptance speech. A few hours before this momentous event, there occurred, according to Dr. Straton, a competition for the Lord's favor. On the one side was the leader of the forces of wickedness, the Governor, for had not Smith told reporters that he had asked "the good Lord" for "propitious weather" for the day of the great ceremonies. On the opposing side was Straton. He had made the issue clear to the Almighty, explaining to Him the manner in which "His preference should be demonstrated. . . ." In view of the moral issues at stake, Straton had implored Heaven to send the rains to wash out, in the literal sense, the opening event of the Democratic campaign. The rains came as Dr. Straton knew they would. Nor did the heavens merely dampen the evil-doers who had gathered to hear their champion. Instead a special sign was given. It appears that Albany alone took a soaking while in all the Republican countryside about New York's capital there were smiling skies. So, to Straton, the big Smith day became "a fizzle in a drizzle." God had revealed, said Straton, a clear "augury of final defeat" for Al Smith.[46] It may be noted that this divine dictate did nothing to lessen the ardor of Dr. Straton to play out his role in that defeat.

CHAPTER SIX

Anti-Catholicism at Flood Stage

> . . . the relations between Catholics and Protestants in this country are a scandal and an offense against Christian charity.[1] —Reinhold Niebuhr

". . . Watch the trains!" The Pope may arrive in person, perhaps on the "north-bound train tomorrow!" So cried a Klansman to a crowd at North Manchester, Indiana.[2] The next day's "north-bound" was met by "some fifteen hundred persons." One hapless passenger looking rather like a cleric had great difficulty in persuading the assembled multitude that he was not in fact the Pope. It is not important whether the details of this episode can be verified. There is no reason to impeach its narrator's conclusion that prejudices which made such Klan appeals politically profitable were "rampant in fully a tenth of Indiana's white, Gentile, Protestant native-born people."[3] Though the Klan's political hold on Indiana was exceeded nowhere, Hoosiers were not altogether different from other Americans.[4]

Some varieties of anti-Catholicism were less direct. A single word or phrase embodying emotionally charged stereotypes could be more effective than shouted admonitions to intercept His Holiness at North Manchester. The most publicized example of the small items likely to inflame opinion was a circular letter which Mrs. Willie W. Caldwell, a Virginia National Committeewoman, wrote to various women in her state, including Mrs. Clara R. Lyon. The letter aimed to inspire and instruct party workers. It contained this paragraph:

> Mr. Hoover himself and the National Committee are depending on the women to save our country in this hour of very vital moral religious crisis. We must save the United States from being Romanized and rum-ridden, and the call is to the women to do something.[5]

Mrs. Lyon was a 1924 La Follette supporter and had been named Republican vice-chairman of her precinct without her knowledge or consent. Her name ought not to have been on Mrs. Caldwell's mailing list. When Mrs. Lyon read the letter she decided it deserved exposure.

Mrs. Caldwell's letter created a considerable stir and prompted Mr. Hoover's most pointed statement on the religious issue. He declared that "Whether this letter is authentic or a forgery it does violence to every instinct that I possess. I resent and repudiate it."[6] Questioned about her letter, Mrs. Caldwell remembered that she had written something about a "very vital moral religious crisis." She recalled nothing in it that referred to Catholicism, nor could she remember using the word "Romanized." She is reported to have said that perhaps her secretary had "dressed up" the letter.[7]

Dr. Hubert Work, Chairman of the Republican National Committee, announced that he had investigated the letter. "I am informed," he said, "that the National Committeewoman did not authorize the introduction of the religious question. . . . The Republican party does not countenance any appeal of this character."[8] So backhanded a treatment of this incident by the Republican National Chairman angered Democrats and did not satisfy all Republicans. There was a widespread conviction that top Republican campaign leaders had been negligent. Senator Carter Glass of Virginia, who had objected strongly to the nomination of Smith, was distressed by the direction party affairs had taken in 1928. He was angered by the poison and misrepresentation that had been poured into the effort to defeat Smith. As Glass saw it, ". . . Mrs. Caldwell was indiscreet enough to write exactly what every Republican campaign whisperer is saying and what many political preachers who traffic in notoriety . . . are proclaiming from platform and pulpit."[9]

Mrs. Caldwell's letter is a clear case of the use of the religious issue in the Republican campaign in Virginia. It may be argued that the word "Romanizing" could be used without conscious thought that the religious issue had thereby been raised. But the credulity of readers should not be imposed upon. If, despite Mrs. Caldwell's own recollection that she had put into her letter something about a "religious crisis," and if the word "Romanized" entered the letter without its author's conscious knowledge, this exemplifies all the more forcefully the power of anti-Catholicism at a time uncomfortably near the present.

Many thought Mr. Hoover was not sufficiently explicit in the several repudiations of bigotry.* Some believed that a word, the right word, by the Republican candidate would have ended the use of the religious issue, at least by officials of the Republican party. Such critics believed that, with a Republican victory so clearly indicated, a more vigorous, case-by-case condemnation of bigotry would have cost the Republican party nothing essential to victory in November. Politicians wish, however, to avoid unnecessary risks even in a "safe" year. This is especially true when, in facing an opponent capable of arousing intense devotion, a gnawing uncertainty accompanies confidence. Yet, Hoover was a very strong candidate, and prosperity was the political prize and possession of the Republican party. With victory so probable, a more frequent and pointed attack on specific examples of the misuse of the religious

* Observers will not agree on the adequacy of the words Mr. Hoover used in his effort to stop the tidal wave of bigotry. An editorial in *The New York Times*, September 30, 1928, suggested that had Theodore Roosevelt been alive he would have followed the course set in his letter of 1908, "branding with hot scorn any American who would allow religious prejudice to affect his vote for President of the United States." It is only just to make two points: first, Hoover did condemn bigotry; second, the temperaments of the two men differed greatly. The *Times* editorial goes on to denounce the circulating of broadsides and pamphlets "which are crawling out of dark corners. . . . Somebody is footing the big bill. Of course, no party committee, high or low, would dare connect itself with this kind of attempt to poison the popular mind, but it is undoubtedly working, and is intended to work for the benefit of the Republican Party."

issue by a number of Republican leaders might have reduced the amount of intolerance in the campaign.

There is no evidence whatsoever that Mr. Hoover trafficked in the whispering campaign. On several occasions he roundly condemned it. He objected strongly to its inherently distorted and immoral character. He singled out the use of the religious issue for special censure. Political as well as moral considerations called for its condemnation, for there could be no certainty that the anti-Catholic campaign would not boomerang. Finally, there is reason to believe that Mr. Hoover was keenly aware of the divisive effects such a campaign could have on postelection America.

Certain of the statements in Mr. Hoover's *Memoirs* on the use of the religious issue are pertinent here. Some of them seem to this writer inadequate as an analysis of the part it played in the campaign of 1928. This in no sense challenges the sincerity of Mr. Hoover's several statements in support of the broad principle of freedom and fair play. The problem was a highly sensitive one, and there was a readiness on the part of Hoover's opponents to misinterpret both his words and his silence. In this respect the candidates were in comparable positions. Unfair and unwarranted deductions were drawn from every reference either of them made to religious prejudice. Hoover was denounced for saying too little, Smith for saying too much. Each candidate repudiated the idea of gaining votes motivated by religious bias. Perhaps more frequent statements by Hoover condemning individual acts of bigotry would not have lessened the torrent of intolerant speech and writing. However, stronger repudiations of specific and illicit uses of Governor Smith's religion might have reduced the total of open anti-Catholic propaganda by some party officials. With one notable exception—the Caldwell incident—Hoover did not both pointedly and publicly repudiate such abuses.

Hoover's *Memoirs* show that he failed to see that the slander directed against him in 1928 was in no way comparable to the vicious and vulgar vilification of Smith.* Mr. Hoover writes:

> The lower rank and file of party workers on both sides did not show the elevation of spirit one could desire.
>
> . . .
>
> The worst plague in the campaign was the religious issue. Governor Smith was the first Presidential candidate of Catholic faith, and for that matter I was the first Quaker. Religion is a difficult matter to handle politically. Even to mention religious questions was enough to fan the flames of bigotry. I tried to stamp out the issue in my acceptance speech on August 11, 1928, by a forthright reference:
>
> "In this land, dedicated to tolerance, we still find outbreaks of intolerance. I come of Quaker stock. My ancestors were persecuted for their beliefs. Here they sought and found religious freedom. By blood and conviction I stand for religious tolerance both in act and in spirit. The glory of our American ideals is the right of every man to worship God according to the dictates of his own conscience."[10]

* Various kinds of unwarranted attacks were made on Hoover in 1928, though the total did not compare with the vicious vilification of him in the 1932 campaign. In 1928 there were some feeble efforts to exploit Mr. Hoover's Quaker religion. There were suggestions that a Quaker could not morally nor constitutionally act as Commander-in-Chief. Unlike the attack on Smith on grounds of dual allegiance, objection to Hoover's religion was inconsequential politically.

According to the Republican candidate:

Governor Smith unwittingly fanned the flame in an address in Oklahoma against intolerance. He insisted that religious faith did not disqualify any man from public office. He was right. But up to that moment it had been an underground issue. The Governor thought that he would gain by bringing it out into the open. The result, however, was to embattle the bigoted Protestants in the open, particularly in the South. I reprimanded many of those who agitated this question.

Hoover then refers to his repudiation of Mrs. Caldwell's letter:

Later in the campaign I said on September 28, with reference to circulars in other parts of the country:

"I cannot fully express my indignation at any such circulars. Nor can I reiterate too strongly that religious questions have no part in this campaign. I have repeatedly stated that neither I nor the Republican party want support on that basis.

"There are important and vital reasons for the return of the Republican administration, but this is not one of them."

Summing up, Mr. Hoover writes:

The issues which defeated the Governor were general prosperity, prohibition, the farm tariffs, Tammany, and the "snuggling" up of the Socialists. Had he been a Protestant, he would certainly have lost and might even have had a smaller vote. An indication of the small importance of the religious issue in final results was the vote in New York State. Here Governor Smith, a Catholic, had been twice elected Governor [Smith was four times elected Governor: 1918, 1922, 1924, and 1926], and therefore no great amount of religious bigotry could have existed. It was for other reasons than this Catholicism that his own state rejected him for President.

Mr. Hoover concludes:

. . . the religious issue had no weight in the final result. I carried all but eight states. In four or five Southern states it may have had weight on my side, although the prohibition and Tammany issues were of far more influence there. As against this the Catholic votes in all states no doubt went preponderantly for Governor Smith, as evidenced by the fact that he carried Massachusetts, traditionally a Republican state, where the Catholics were stronger than in any other state in the Union.[11]

A general demurrer must be entered against much of this conclusion. Recalling that such issues as Tammany, Prohibition, and religion cannot be appraised in separate compartments, some of Mr. Hoover's remarks cannot be accurately tested, but they still lack probability. It is one thing to concede that the power exerted by the Catholic issue cannot be measured precisely, but this in no way validates Mr. Hoover's conclusion that "the religious issue had no weight in the final result." Even in the State of New York there is evidence that Smith's religious affiliation was a major reason, though by no means the only reason, why many would not support him for the presidency.

Shortly before Labor Day, when the formal campaign speechmaking was about to begin, Chairman Work addressed himself, under pressure from the opposition, to the problem of the whispering campaign. He promised a "clean fight." Work's pledge was an answer to a challenge in vice-presidential candidate Robinson's acceptance speech.[12] Robinson had denounced the slanderous charges that Smith was a "drunkard." He condemned those who whispered that the Governor's election would mean "priest rule." He stressed Smith's excellent record in support of the public schools of New York, and he praised the fairness of his appointments. Smith, said Senator Robinson, "has not been a Catholic Governor."[13] Robinson insisted that his ticket mate had conclusively demonstrated his devotion to the principle of the separation of church and state. For the next two months, Senator Robinson pleaded with southern and western audiences for tolerance, but these pleas were unavailing. The printing and dissemination of anti-Catholic leaflets and cartoons increased in volume.

Though religious propaganda in politics was often crudely expressed, it would be a mistake to assume that for that reason it was ineffective. The notorious and vicious "oath" of the Knights of Columbus cropped up all over the United States. This spurious document was not invented in 1928, but had appeared periodically to bolster anti-Catholicism. In 1913 it was read into the *Congressional Record*[14] in a fraudulent election contest in which the loser presented evidence of its use against him. It appeared occasionally in the next decade, often after 1923. In 1928 it was spread over the front pages of leaflets and broadsides,* appeared in abbreviated form beneath lurid pictures showing Protestants hung from trees by Catholics, was placed in rural mail boxes by Klansmen, and in most instances passed freely through the mails. Dr. Henry van Dyke, famed author and Presbyterian clergyman, found ten copies in a single mail delivery.[17] Sometimes the ill-informed, appalled

*The *Florida Cracker*, published weekly at Jacksonville, reproduced the spurious "oath" on page one of its first issue, September 15, 1928.[15] The editor of this weekly was also chairman of publicity for the Republican party in Florida.[16]

—despite their anti-Catholic prejudices—at the enormity of the charges against Catholics, asked their leaders whether the "oath" were accurate. Sometimes an affirmative answer was disingenuously or ignorantly implied in responses which referred questioners back to the source, the *Congressional Record*, whose every word was presumed by the uninformed to be true.

There were many indignant charges that the United States Post Office Department had in effect become a partner in the dissemination of anti-Catholic propaganda. Occasionally there were announcements that the Department had seized anti-Catholic leaflets and post cards. As a rule slanderous propaganda flowed through the mails although there were Department rulings barring certain anti-Catholic materials "where the attacks were of a personal nature and were plain on the outside of mail. . . ."[18] The problem was a difficult one;* there was nothing unique about it in 1928 except the tremendous volume and ugly nature of the propaganda.

Did the Republican National Committee make a calculated decision to exploit the religious issue? The

* A letter from Roy C. Frank, Solicitor, Post Office Department, points to the difficulty of the problem: ". . . there is no postal law which forbids use of the mails for attacks upon religious groups, per se. . . ." The pertinent provision, now found in Section 36.4(b), Postal Laws and Regulations of 1948, 18 U. S. Code, 1718, provides sanctions of $1,000 in fine or a year's imprisonment, or both. But most of the defamatory post cards and leaflets indicated no source. Probably the most notoriously anti-Catholic of all such papers were *The Fellowship Forum*, a Klan organ published in the nation's capital, and *The New Menace*, published in Aurora, Missouri.

charge was repeated throughout the campaign, but it has never been proved. However, some Republican party officials and some bolting Democrats made little effort to stop the use of that issue. There is, in addition, proof that Republican party leaders in a number of southern states were guilty of exploiting Smith's religion for political ends.*[19]

Alabama will serve as an example. In no state was there more open use of Catholicism as a political issue. The unblushing spokesman was Oliver D. Street, chairman of the Republican state campaign committee. Street defied important local newspaper opposition in deliberately making Smith's religion a formal part of the campaign in Alabama. He covered the state that sent Heflin to the Senate with anti-Catholic propaganda in the form of a notorious four-page circular. In it Street declared: ". . . the Catholic Church and Governor Smith's membership in it legitimately enter into this campaign as a very live and vital issue."[20]

The cultural level of Street's circular was much below that of Charles Marshall's 1927 challenge to Smith, but he used Marshall's main argument. He used the direct approach in appealing to Alabama Democrats to bolt their Catholic nominee. There seemed never to be any lack of money to carry forward this or similar attacks on Smith's religion. Pro-Smith groups were confident that the money must have been supplied by National Republican headquarters. Typical of the perpetrators of such documents, Street denied that his cir-

* The campaign in the South was under the direct supervision of Colonel H. A. Mann.

cular was an attack on religion. He magnanimously granted Smith the right to worship as he pleased, but he repeated the cliché about "ring kissing." The circular cited the scope of Catholic activities especially in the very recent past—the Eucharistic Congress in Chicago in 1926 and Smith's rejoinder to Marshall's onslaught. Smith's answer to Marshall simply demonstrated, according to Street, that the Governor was the tool of Father Duffy and the hierarchy.

The Republican National Chairman, Dr. Work, sent Republican State Chairman Street a telegram of rebuke. Street told reporters he had not received it. He boasted he had distributed 200,000 copies of his circular. The final figure apparently was much higher. It is not recorded that Mr. Hoover made any specific public comment on Street's handiwork.

The response of the Republican high command to violations by Republican officials of Mr. Hoover's warning against use of the religious issue varied. For example, the official Republican attitude toward Mrs. Caldwell's "Romanizing" letter had been a mixture of rebuke and an unwillingness to admit that the letter had introduced the religious issue into the campaign. No official effort was made to persuade the electorate that the following passage from Republican Chairman Street's circular did not directly introduce the religious issue into the Alabama campaign:

> . . . the time has not yet arrived when his church deems it expedient to make an issue with Gov. Smith himself. His church will use him as an instrument to bring about conditions

when it will be expedient to make the issue. Then it will make the issue with Gov. Smith himself, and if he does not yield it will crush him, as it has crushed thousands of others, as ruthlessly as it would crush a Protestant.

Gov. Smith may believe he would be strong enough to resist the tremendous pressure that his institution is capable at any time of exerting upon him or any other Roman Catholic. Hundreds of thousands of stronger men morally than Gov. Smith have found themselves, when the test came, unable to resist.[21]

It was common practice to associate religion with one or more other issues that formed parts of the social campaign within the campaign of 1928. For example, religion was occasionally linked with the antisegregationist stand of the Catholic church. The threat to white supremacy supposedly inherent in a Smith victory was a constant theme. Race consciousness was scandalously exploited by both parties. The partial success of the Hoover forces in undermining the historic role of the Democratic party as the guarantor of white supremacy merits attention in the longer view of the felt relationship of the Democratic party to the preservation of the South's local customs. In the Deep South the Republicans usually posed as champions of the "lily-white" cause. A picture of a prominent Harlem politician dictating to a white secretary was very widely distributed and was used in an effort to convince southern Democrats that the northern wing of the party of Jefferson and Jefferson Davis had betrayed the South and was no longer capable of guaranteeing white supremacy. Democrats, however, had no cause for self-congratulation. Like their opponents they dipped low in the bag of political tricks, representing Mr. Hoover as a threat to southern institutions.

The maintenance of racial segregation was loudly proclaimed by some of the clergy. High-powered evangelists and sensational preachers, in contradistinction to thousands of clergymen who tried to avoid emotional methods, used the race issue in a manner that differed little from the way some extremist politicians have traditionally exploited it. Some Democrats who bolted Smith helped spread the impression that the northern Democracy was in bondage to the politically important Negro population.*

Snobbery was an important component of the social campaign of 1928. Smith was its victim. Mischief and meanness reached a low point when invidious remarks and innuendoes were made about "the Al Smiths." This was such a common and significant part of the campaign that, though distasteful, some notice of it is unavoidable. Nor is this a phase of the campaign that can be made vivid by generalizations. Two examples will suffice; they must stand for unnumbered others. The Houston *Chronicle* reports that in addressing a meeting of the W.C.T.U. in Houston, Mrs. Florence T. Griswold, Republican National Committeewoman for Texas, made the following remarks:

* Senator Simmons of North Carolina illustrated this in the following suggestion: "There is a negro paper published in New York known as The National Crusader. It is a strong Smith paper. It might pay to have someone subscribe to that so as to keep up with what they are doing in the matter of organizing Smith clubs of this race in the North."[22]

> . . . the pope missed something by not hearing me speak this morning, and if he could see these women before me now, see how things are going in Texas, he would know it was no use. . . .
>
> Can you imagine Al Smith in the White House?
> Can you imagine Mrs. Smith in the White House?
> Can you imagine an aristocratic foreign Ambassador saying to her, "What a charming gown," and the reply, "You said a 'mouthful!' "

According to the account, "shrieks of laughter and applause" greeted this reflection upon Mrs. Smith.[23]

Another and well-publicized example of snobbery came freely and doubtlessly with no ill will, from William Allen White. Interviewed in July in New York, White's words were reported as follows:

> "There will be more mention of the words 'social' and 'economics' in the White House with Hoover," he said. "Hoover can talk upon any subject. If you ask him about Italian primitives I'm sure he'd have something to say. And he knows that Leonardo da Vinci is something other than the name of a cigar." . . .
>
> "But wouldn't the words 'social' and 'economics' be mentioned in the White House with Al Smith there?" Mr. White was asked.
> "I'm not so sure," he said.
> "Well, at least if Al Smith doesn't mention them, don't you think those who surround him would?"
> "You mean Fourteenth Street?"
> "No—Mrs. Moscowitz [*sic*], Judge Proskauer, Judge Cardozo." [24]

White conceded that perhaps such civilizing human agencies would be in evidence but indicated that he considered the Republican candidate by far the better cultural risk.

One must admire Smith's refusal to be other than himself. This applied to his conduct during the campaign of 1928. His campaign theme song, "The Sidewalks of New York," was played wherever he spoke. The brown derby was almost always in evidence. Apparently this sartorial symbol was of doubtful political usefulness outside the large cities. We are told that at Oklahoma City the derby and "The Sidewalks of New York" caused a great deal of comment. Several North Carolinians have told the writer that the brown derby did not help Smith's cause in the Tar Heel state.

One southerner denied that snobbery had anything to do with his section's opposition to the "Happy Warrior." What was termed snobbery, he wrote, was much more than a distaste for the New Yorker's " 'brown derby' Yaller shoes, gold tooth smile, and other sartorial adornments."

The writer continued:

> . . . I think we would all naturally prefer a man of high culture and character, such as Woodrow Wilson, for president, to a product of the slums of New York with only a Tammany training, and whose highest ambition is to see the time come when he can put his foot on the brass rail and blow the foam off again. This is no "bologny talk" either, are we not told daily that he is honest and means what he says. Just compare this high ambition with that of Woodrow Wilson to establish a League of Nations to prevent war.[25]

Smith was sneeringly dismissed as a product of the "Fulton Fishmarket." (This species of honest employment did not enter into our political romance along with rail-splitting.) Smith was accused of using the language of the "Bowery tough." A considerable part of the

Characteristic of many anti-Smith cartoons, this crudity from The Fellowship Forum, *November 3, 1928, proclaimed Smith's unworthiness to fill Wilson's shoes. (New York State Library, Albany)*

condescension seems to have been based on a falsification of Smith's personal life and on the quality of his voice over the "raddio." An educator wrote Senator Norris that he was "very much grieved . . . I listened to Al in his Denver speech. I watched him closely," he said. "I doubt his sincerity and certainly he is not a man of deep learning."[26] Radio was now an important campaign technique, undoubtedly to Smith's disadvantage. According to one auditor, Hoover passed the radio test, but there was "pure political 'boloney' [*sic*] in the tones of Mr. Smith."[27]

There were ridiculous charges that on grounds of lack of sobriety Smith's personal habits made him a poor White House risk. This impression of the Governor was whispered and broadcast widely. It was said that in rural areas some of Smith's fellow religionists credited the charge. A southerner wrote Senator Simmons that it was a mistake to suppose that all Catholics would vote for Smith. ". . . One Roman Catholic lady said she would be afraid for him to occupy the White House because of his inability to control his appetite for drink—that she would be afraid he would do something to bring disgrace upon the Roman Catholic Church. . . ."[28] This scarcely reflected the views of millions of Al Smith's city champions.

If economic and political problems were often subordinated to the colorful, emotion-stirring issues such as Prohibition, religion, race, and snobbery, many were convinced that the activities of the Protestant churches were chiefly responsible. Partly because of the unworthy way in which not a few ministers conducted themselves in 1928, it has become fashionable to condemn out of hand "political parsons." A balanced and fair appraisal of the values the churches were determined to save by entering politics is needed. The abusive treatment of Governor Smith by many church people was often un-Christian, but Protestantism has been blamed for some deeds that ought to be laid at other doors. The churches did not create the Klan. Klansmen tried to enhance their prestige by patronizing and "protecting" Protestantism. When anti-Prohibitionism seemed to ardent drys to have become incarnate in Al Smith and his possible election loomed as a menace to the years of labor which had culminated in the Eighteenth Amendment, many religious leaders felt that, to safeguard their country against a return of the saloon, full-scale political action was required. And so they entered politics.

There is ample evidence that Prohibition, though vastly important, was not the only reason why the churches plunged into politics in 1928. Broadly speaking, what was believed to be in danger was "Anglo-Saxon civilization." It was assumed that Protestantism was a mainstay of that undefined way of life. Roman Catholicism was regarded as belonging to an alien way, inimical to the preservation of the best in the American past. Methodist Bishop Edwin D. Mouzon wrote:[29]

> . . . the present time offers a good opportunity for preachers in a constructive way to present to a public almost totally uninformed touching such matters, a series of sermons setting forth the essential difference between Roman Catholicism and Protestantism. In preparation of such a series of sermons, I

suggest that our Methodist preachers turn to our Twenty-five Articles of Religion and study again those articles which set forth the historic protest of Evangelical Christianity against the errors of Rome. . . .*

Bishop Mouzon's optimism in believing that such subjects "would offer a great opportunity for kindly and constructive preaching" was excessive in the context of the conditions existing in 1928. This is true even though he ruled out "books written by former priests and escaped nuns."[31]

The Bishops of the Methodist Church, South, were spectacularly divided on the part the Methodist church should or should not play in the campaign. Bishops James Cannon, Jr., John M. Moore, Horace M. DuBose, and Edwin D. Mouzon stood for active participation; Bishop Warren A. Candler, greatly respected senior Bishop of the Church and Bishop Collins Denny made statements in opposition. The strong stand of the aged

* The Bishop passed on to Methodist ministers the following suggestions for sermon topics:

1. Romanism, the Religion of External Authority; Protestantism, the Religion of the Spirit.
2. The Spiritual Authority of the Bible versus the Dead Hand of Traditionalism.
3. The Priesthood of All Believers; or the Right of the Individual to Come to God Without the Intermediation of a Priest.
4. Salvation Through Faith in Christ Rather Than Through Belief in Creed.
5. The Ethical Emphasis of Protestantism as Against the Sacramentarianism of Rome.
6. Church and State in Roman Catholic and in Protestant Teaching.
7. The Miracles of the New Testament and Roman Catholic Pseudo-Miracles.
8. The Duty of the Church to Interest Itself in Public Morals.[30]

Bishop Candler against using the pulpit for political ends is credited with keeping many of the clergy from actively engaging in political activities.[32] On September 8, at Richmond, Virginia, 133 persons, some of them members of the Methodist church, met and condemned the policy of the majority of the bishops.[33]

Tension was great and feeling ran high. There were prophecies that the ministers would drive a wedge between themselves and their congregations. The unpublished correspondence of some southerners reinforces the impression of a badly divided people. So bitter and so personal were many of the charges that focused on Smith's candidacy that some carry-over of bitterness after election day was inevitable. The views of many southern lawyers and journalists appear to have been much at variance with those of the majority of clergymen. While there were, of course, many Protestant laymen whose views and actions in this campaign ran parallel with those of the clergy, many southerners were genuinely convinced that their pastors were leading the churches to new and dangerous ground.

The lot of the preachers who hoped to avoid use of their pulpits for political purposes was a difficult one. There were many such clergymen. The Reverend Dr. J. E. Hicks, Baptist minister in Baltimore, read his congregation parts of a letter from a southern preacher who hoped "that you are not cursed in Baltimore with the same kind of political hysteria as we have down here. What is a preacher to do? Some of them are in danger of losing their pulpits if they preach politics—and some of them if they do not. . . ."[34]

Some laymen refused any part in a crusade for deliverance from evil through a campaign of slander and hate. Senator Lee S. Overman, one of North Carolina's leading statesmen, addressed himself in a private letter to those voters who "openly placed their opposition to Governor Smith on the ground of his religion, while still others opposed him on that ground but do not openly say so." Convinced that the fear of a Catholic President was ill grounded and that the "No-Popery" rumors were ridiculous, Senator Overman recalled:

For fifty years the Pope himself has carried on a futile fight to get his pitifully few acres in the Vatican extended, and if he cannot affect the Italian government, how in the name of common-sense can he make you and me kiss his toe?[35]

Overman was convinced that the whispering campaign against Smith was "directed largely to his religion." He deplored the fire-eating tactics of "certain Methodist bishops and ministers scattering hatred and prejudice. . . ." He believed that

. . . most of them seek to justify themselves on the grounds that they are fighting a moral fight for temperance. But the teachings of Christ convince me that it were better to have wine in the belly than hatred in the heart . . . I deplore the intemperate words and acts of those who seek to defeat Smith by spreading hatred among us. The fanatics who do so will hurt Prohibition more than they will help it, and I fear the Bishops and Ministers above referred will, if they have not already, done harm to our beloved old Church and raised such bitterness as will take years to eradicate.[36]

Families were often split in 1928. One North Carolinian wrote, "We are having a most heart breaking

"THE AL SMITHS! OH, MY *DEAR!*"

There is no better illustration of the part played by snobbery in the campaign than this cartoon by Rollin Kirby in the New York World, *September 7, 1928. (Press Publishing Company)* time, Brother is fighting brother, father fighting son, and husbands fighting wives. . . ."[37]

A prolonged battle on the live topic of the proper relations between the religious and political orders was waged in both the secular and the religious press. The practical and immediate decision of church leaders, that duty clearly demanded all-out participation in the political arena in 1928, was reached because politics seemed the sole means of safeguarding the moral order. Whether viewed in its special social aspects—Prohibition, Tammany, and Romanism—or as a comprehensive whole, the determination to save "Anglo-Saxon civilization" in this campaign was unique. To defeat Smith was called both a moral and a religious duty. The election of Hoover was often viewed more as a means to that end than as the end itself. In their view of Smith as the symbol of many evils, it would have been surprising had evangelical Protestants confined their main efforts in 1928 to the preaching of "Christ and Him crucified." The great harm flowed less from a violation of anyone's theory about the relation of religious to political institutions than from the fact that so much of the activity carried on in the name of religion was done with "hatred in the heart."

Battle plans for the role which the church would play were prepared long before Smith won the nomination. Clear warnings of the storm ahead were sounded as far back as 1923. By early 1928 the nature, though not the full intensity, of the anti-Smith movement within Protestantism was clearly foreshadowed. In May, 1928, when it seemed improbable that the Smith bandwagon could be stopped at Houston, four thousand delegates of the Southern Baptist church pledged opposition to any wet who might be nominated for President. This was typical of the thought and planned action of sister denominations.

Though there were more Baptists than Methodists in the South, it is a Methodist Bishop, James Cannon, who will be remembered as the driving force in organizing the battle of southern Protestantism against Al Smith. Bishop Cannon, more than anyone else, was probably responsible for the failure of the Democratic party to hold the line for Smith in the Upper South and in Texas and Florida.[38] Early in 1928 the Bishop, a life-long Democrat, decided that preparations must be made to cope with a Smith nomination. The essential thing was to convince southerners that they must split their ballots against Smith if he should win the nomination. This, said Cannon, would be done "altogether apart from his religion, although I knew that he was the intolerant, bigoted type characteristic of the Irish Roman Catholic hierarchy of New York City."[39]

Immediately after Smith's nomination Cannon, acting with the Baptist leader, Dr. A. J. Barton, issued a call for a conference of dry southern Democrats to meet at Asheville, North Carolina, to shift the anti-Smith drive into high gear. The conference, meeting on July 18, was a monumental success. It launched a great campaign of propaganda to convince faithful Protestant, Democratic drys that the election of Hoover was not only morally necessary but was wholly consonant with the ultimate revival of the historic Democratic party. The conference adjourned "in seeming confidence that nearly every southern state would . . . repudiate the betrayal of the Democratic party [which, according to Dr. Barton] . . . has been delivered to the tender mercies of the Tammany tiger whose teeth and claws are red with political blood of every Democratic candidate for a generation."[40] A suitable organization was established at Richmond, Virginia, to do the political job that lay ahead. Bishop Cannon was in practical command.*

It would be an egregious error to suppose that the candidate's religion did not enter importantly into the thoughts and words of many of those who waged so fierce a fight against Al Smith. The Methodists were perhaps the most active in the crusade to defeat Smith, but the Baptists with their great numbers, the Presbyterians with their considerable influence, and the Lutherans with their very frank opposition to Smith as a Catholic kept pace with the Methodists in the anti-Catholic procession. But Bishop Cannon's part in the campaign, together with the prominence of the Methodist Board of Temperance, Prohibition and Public

* It is not necessary to retell the story of Bishop Cannon's record as a financier or his spectacular difficulties with the lay and ecclesiastical courts after 1928. Cannon possessed very real genius as an organizer and planner. He was dead set on the defeat of Smith and was willing to finance his campaign for that object by funds from convenient sources. Asked whether he would accept money from the Republican National Committee, the Bishop is alleged to have replied, "Certainly. I never look a gift horse in the mouth."[41] On one occasion he received $50,000 from a New Yorker who donated the sum with the object of carrying Virginia for Hoover.[42]

Morals, explains the conviction of some that Methodists were somehow rather uniquely intolerant.

A Methodist who was particularly zealous in the cause of defeating Smith was Deets Pickett, Research Secretary for *The Voice*, a monthly organ of the Methodist Board of Temperance, Prohibition and Public Morals. More than a fortnight before the Asheville conference, Pickett had warned a congregation at Cherrydale, Virginia:

. . . Give a Tammany man one term in office as President and the entire government service will be "salted" with creatures of that organization. Your kind of people will not have a look-in, Civil Service or no Civil Service, for so much as a stenographer's position in government service, unless you are willing to be that convenient thing, a Methodist or Baptist tool of Tammany.

Lest the point be missed, the Research Secretary expanded on this subject of religion:

. . . The merest suggestion of opposition to Al Smith is denounced with vile abuse and when one goes so far as to question even in the slightest degree the influence of the Roman Catholic Church upon the government, he is shouted down with cries of "Intolerance," and "Bigotry." Those words do not answer honest questions. Friends of Smith can call me intolerant or a bigot if they wish; I will not be deterred by abuse from exercising my right as a free American citizen. . . .

Mr. Pickett admitted that there were some trustworthy Catholic public servants of "transcendent" character. Basing his attack on the argument that a Catholic conscience was, nonetheless, undependable, he restated and vulgarized Marshall's dual allegiance challenge to Smith.

Pickett's words illustrate the point that what might have been expected from the soapbox spellbinder was very often uttered from the pulpit in 1928:

These are questions, ladies and gentlemen, which abuse will no longer answer. They must be answered frankly in understandable English and that answer must come from St. Peter's or from the hierarchy, before the American people are satisfied. I know that Gov. Smith has made an answer, but an answer needing a lawyer for its interpretation, but he made his best answer when he knelt like a flunkey at the feet of the papal delegate, humiliating the great state which has honored him by election to the governor's chair. Personally, I want to say here and now that my people quit kissing hands in 1776 and I don't intend to resume the practice and I may be permitted perhaps to have a contempt for anyone who does.

At the conclusion of the address, "every person came to the platform and expressed approval."[43]

In discussing bigotry, it is all too easy to suppose that what happened in the South was unique to that section. Actually much of what happened in the South was typical of what occurred elsewhere. For example, the Methodist church, through its Board of Temperance, Prohibition and Public Morals and its Research Secretary, made a nationwide, not just southern, fight to defeat Smith. Mr. Pickett planned some forty-odd Methodist conferences before election day. In mid-September he told the Erie, Pennsylvania, conference:

"It is demanded that you violate your conscience, that you repudiate your convictions, that you pass under the yoke of Tammany, never again to return to freedom, so that your children, if they be Democrats, shall hereafter be only hewers of wood and drawers of water for such men as Olvany, Brenan, Proskauer."

He followed this with an old-fashioned attack on the Pope.[44]

The Presbyterians found themselves in an intradenominational fracas after the Moderator of the General Assembly, Dr. Hugh K. Walker, directed a plea in the *Presbyterian Magazine*, the official monthly, to all churchmen to "fight to the bitter end the election of Alfred E. Smith. . . ." There was vigorous protest against Walker's presumption by such leading Presbyterians as Breckenridge Long and a former moderator, Dr. Henry van Dyke.* The latter charged that Walker was doing what he accused the Pope of doing.[46]

Perhaps of all the larger denominations Lutherans opposed Smith most unequivocally on dogmatic lines. The National Lutheran Editors' Association decided, two weeks before Smith took the religious issue to the people at Oklahoma City, that Lutheran papers "will not and need not advise their readers how to vote," but the editors so emphasized the dual allegiance charges—"the peculiar allegiance that a faithful Catholic owes . . . a foreign sovereign . . ."—that they could safely leave action to the "conscientious judgment" of fellow Lutherans.[47]

Few incidents during the campaign aroused more indignation than the story that the Democratic Chairman, John J. Raskob, was encouraging a revolt by

* Three weeks earlier Dr. van Dyke, who worked stalwartly to stop bigotry in this campaign, scathingly condemned those who circulated pamphlets that insisted there was an "unwritten law" against a Catholic President. He referred particularly to the work of the anonymous E. A. (see p. 29), initials which he thought possibly stood for Evidently Absurd.[45]

wealthy southern laymen against anti-Smith clergymen. Raskob's trouble began with inept handling of a press conference. Commenting on reports that serious trouble was brewing for the party in the South, Raskob expressed optimism. This he based partly on reports that economic pressure would be applied to correct the ways of the "political parsons." *The New York Times* reported Raskob's remarks as follows:

> I think there is nothing in the South that need give us cause for alarm. From the analysis we make they show more religious prejudice than anything else, the sort of bigotry than can be easily dispelled. Some of the Methodists are serving notice upon the Church, its officials and others who are trying to inject the religious issue into the campaign, saying that they must stop or they will cease to contribute to the Church."
>
> Mr. Raskob said he had been told that there was quite a movement in the South among the Methodists, protesting against dragging the Church into politics and threatening to withdraw their financial support.
>
> "It is just gossip that I have got from Southern people," Mr. Raskob said.[48]

The story of Raskob's alleged threats against the southern ministers was retold, with embellishments, during the next three months. Senator Heflin accused Raskob of a ". . . bold and brazen effort to muzzle the Protestant preachers of the South . . ."

> The plan boldly announced is to call on Democratic members of the various Protestant churches in the South to refuse to give financial support to Protestant preachers who cannot conscientiously support Governor Smith. This bold and brazen attempt to tell Protestant preachers of the South that they will not be permitted to do the right as God gives them the light to see the right is an effort to chain the Southern

Protestant preachers' conscience to the Roman-Tammany chariot wheels.[49]

No speaker before church groups was so much in demand and none was so controversial as a woman member of the Coolidge administration, Mrs. Mabel Walker Willebrandt. An Assistant Attorney General of the United States, assigned to Prohibition enforcement, Mrs. Willebrandt was on a kind of informal lend-lease arrangement for talks before church conferences or meetings. She talked about Prohibition, Tammany Hall, evils of New York City, and the iniquitous nomination the Democrats made at Houston. The important fact is that many of her speeches were made before strictly denominational groups. Depending upon the commentator, Mabel Willebrandt was either the savior of American morality or the brash disturber of hallowed ideas about the separation of church and state. Her enemies alleged that, without directly referring to Smith's religion, other than by denying that she was the administration's agent for marshaling Protestants behind Hoover, she violated most of the basic amenities of political campaigning. Her critics were plainly of the opinion that if the Eighteenth Amendment had to be championed by so unpalatable a product of the Nineteenth, both of these recent addenda to the fundamental law ought to be repealed posthaste.

What was the special quality of Mrs. Willebrandt's part in the campaign that brought both paeans of praise and loud demands that she be gagged? By taking to the stump, she unquestionably aimed to enforce the Eighteenth Amendment. To do this, she campaigned hard against Al Smith and for the man who believed the purpose of the Amendment was "noble."

Mrs. Willebrandt's speeches need not be detailed. She was in the thick of the battle by Labor Day. Her speech at Springfield, Ohio, on September 7, was a direct appeal for Methodists to enter the fight for Hoover. It was made to delegates, lay and clerical, to the Ohio Methodist Conference. Mrs. Willebrandt denounced "willful sections" of the United States. Her special scorn was saved for New York City and its speakeasies. She called upon Methodists throughout the land to join the Hoover crusade.

> There are 2,000 pastors here. You have in your churches more than 600,000 members of the Methodist Church in Ohio alone. That is enough to swing the election. The 600,000 have friends in others States. Write to them. Every day and every ounce of your energy are needed to rouse the friends of prohibition to register and vote.[50]

Most accounts suggest that Mrs. Willebrandt thoroughly enjoyed her role. The explosive character of her activities was something to worry the Republican National Committee but, as the sequel showed, it was not possible for the high command to make a successful disengagement even if that had been judged the wise course. Mrs. Willebrandt's use of the churches during the middle two weeks of September, together with Governor Smith's September 20 speech in which he castigated her by name, changed the tempo and emphasis of the campaign. Mrs. Willebrandt for a time reduced Senator Borah, leading Republican speaker on political

THE PINCH HITTER

Assistant Attorney General Mabel Willebrandt's "unofficial" role in the campaign is here expressed in baseball terms. (Fitzpatrick, St. Louis Post-Dispatch, *September 28, 1928.)*

and economic issues, to a subordinate role. As tempers rose and as the Republican National Committee squirmed in the face of insistent demands for a clear definition of Mrs. Willebrandt's status, ominous charges were made by Democrats that the Republicans, through Mrs. Willebrandt, were now officially, if obliquely, stirring religious prejudices. Not all Republicans were satisfied with the Willebrandt chapter in this campaign. The defense, exceedingly lame, included denials and half-denials that Mrs. Willebrandt had official party status. It included, too, loud countercharges that Smith was preparing to use the Willebrandt affair as the occasion for an all-out, open bid for support on the religious issue.

Mrs. Willebrandt's direct appeal to the churches was but one of many efforts to align the Protestant forces of the country in a militant formation against the Democratic candidate. But the focusing of public attention on the personality and methods of Mrs. Willebrandt and the fact that she was an employee of the Republican administration made her speeches, more than any other single episode, the catalytic agent that influenced Governor Smith to decide to bring the religious issue into the open by devoting a major campaign address to it.

The day following Mrs. Willebrandt's speech before the Ohio Methodists, New York's Mayor Jimmy Walker, who like most New Yorkers bore no love for Mrs. Willebrandt, conferred with Smith. As he emerged from that meeting, the dapper mayor blasted those who were responsible for the widely circulated charge that Governor Smith had favored Catholics in making appointments. The New York *Herald Tribune* was now certain that Smith and his advisers had decided to try to squeeze political advantage from the religious issue.

> First they will try to arouse public indignation and then to turn the indignation against the Republican ticket in an effort to duplicate the 1884 reaction to the "Rum, Romanism, and Rebellion" cry that is credited with having defeated James G. Blaine.[51]

Smith's enemies feared he might succeed in turning to his advantage the attacks on his religion. The Governor kept his own counsel, refusing to divulge whether or not he would talk about religion in his forthcoming western tour. There seems to have been no unanimity among his advisers on the best course to follow in a matter so fraught with political danger.

The tone of the account in the *Herald Tribune* was sure to arouse suspicions about Governor Smith's motives. The *Tribune* would not admit that the anti-Smith whispering campaign was an ugly reality. Governor Smith was depicted as about to perform some sort of self-serving trick by injecting the religious issue into the campaign.*

The high point of the drama of anti-Catholicism in the campaign came on September 20. That night Governor Smith spoke at Oklahoma City to an audience

* The Smith *Papers* make it entirely clear that, with the cooperation of people from all parts of the United States, he was kept abreast of the campaign of personal vilification against him. It was a gratuitous and uncalled-for assumption to suppose, as was constantly asserted by his opponents, that Smith's decision to make open reply, at Oklahoma City, was a conscienceless trick.

including the Reverend John Roach Straton and many who shared his views. Oklahoma's former Senator Robert L. Owen had bolted the Smith ticket, publicly denouncing the "Tammany candidate." The Klan was still powerful in Oklahoma, anti-Catholic feeling was widespread, and there was tension in the air when Smith with his party paraded through the city streets. There was real concern for Smith's personal safety, and his eastern advisers were relieved when the telephone brought word that the Governor had reached his hotel safely after an emotion-packed evening.

Smith began this notable address, unique in the history of presidential campaign speeches, with an attack on Owen, who had made the mistake of belittling Smith's outstanding political record. In reply Smith read glowing tributes from some outstanding members of both parties—Charles Evans Hughes, Nicholas Murray Butler, Robert Lansing, Virginia G. Gildersleeve. Asked Smith:

> Do Senator Owen and the forces behind him know more about my record than these distinguished men and women who have watched it and studied it? But Senator Owen and his kind are not sincere. They know that this Tammany cry is an attempt to drag a red herring across the trail.

The Governor denounced as false apostles of Americanism those who had flagrantly misrepresented the record of his political appointments:

> One lie widely circulated, particularly through the Southern part of the country, is that during my Governorship I appointed practically nobody to office but members of my own church.

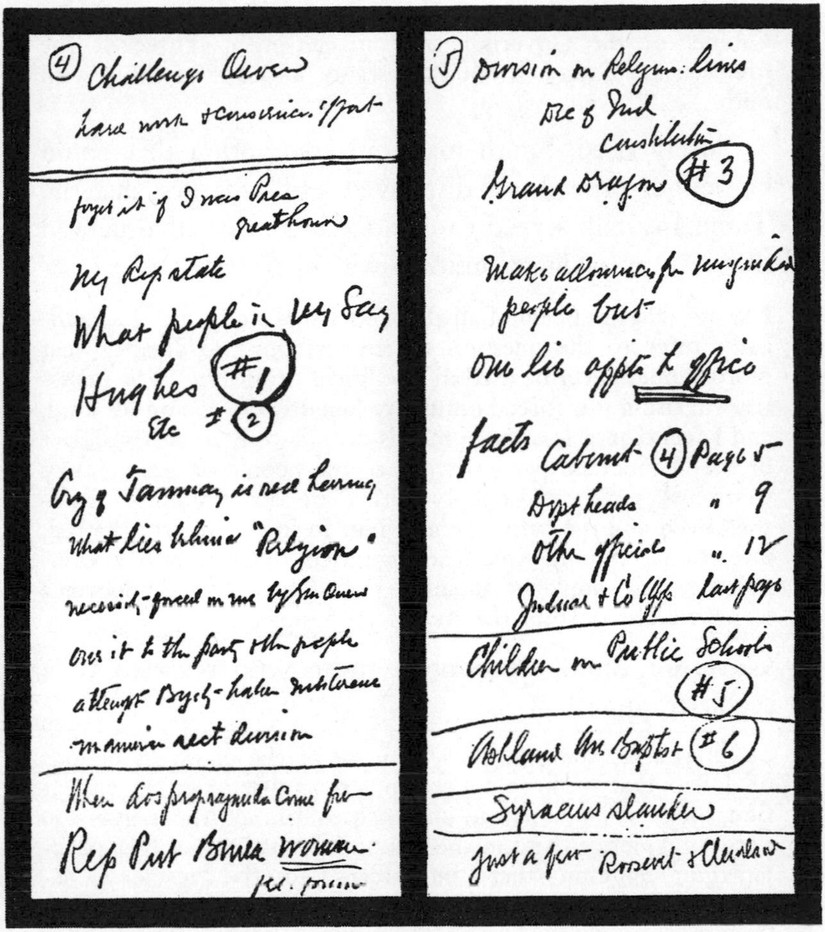

These notes in Smith's handwriting were prepared for his speech at Oklahoma City, September 20, 1928, in which he first took official notice of the religious issue. Such jottings on the backs of envelopes were typical. (Museum of the City of New York)

What are the facts? On investigation I find that in the Cabinet of the Governor sit fourteen men. Three of the fourteen are Catholics, ten Protestants, and one of the Jewish faith. . . .*

Sorely tried, Smith made an assumption that could be neither proved nor disproved. He charged that the Tammany talk served to camouflage a deeper issue and that an unmasking operation was in order:

I know what lies behind all this and I shall tell you. I specifically refer to the question of my religion. Ordinarily that word should never be used in a political campaign. The necessity for using it is forced on me by Senator Owen and his kind, and I feel that at least once in this campaign I, as the candidate of the Democratic party, owe it to the people of this country to discuss frankly and openly with them this attempt of Senator Owen and the forces behind him to inject bigotry, hatred, intolerance and un-American sectarian division into a campaign which should be an intelligent debate of the important issues which confront the American people.

Governor Smith denounced those who resorted to a sectarian appeal:

. . . it is a sad thing in 1928, in view of the countless billions of dollars that we have poured into the cause of public education, to see some American citizens proclaiming themselves 100 percent American and in the document that makes that proclamation suggesting that I be defeated for the Presidency because of my religious belief.

* No lie about Smith was more widely broadcast, by post card, Klan publications, and gossip, than the assertion that the Governor appointed chiefly Catholics and Jews to state offices. Collections of letters and clippings abound with examples; the whispering and the knowing nods that certainly accompanied the proliferation of such charges must be left to the reader's imagination. In asking for contributions for the party, Democratic Treasurer James W. Gerard had printed on the reverse side of the appeal card a tabulation of Smith's appointments by religious affiliation.

The grand dragon of the realm of Arkansas, writing to a citizen of that state, urges my defeat because I am a Catholic and in the letter suggests to the man, who happened to be a delegate to the Democratic Convention, that by voting against me he was upholding American ideals and institutions as established by our forefathers.

. . .

Nothing could be so out of line with the spirit of America. Nothing could be so foreign to the teachings of Jefferson. Nothing could be so contradictory of our whole history. Nothing could be so false to the teachings of our divine Lord himself. The world knows no greater mockery than the use of the blazing cross, the cross upon which Christ died, as a symbol to instill into the hearts of men a hatred of their brethren, while Christ preached and died for the love and brotherhood of man.

. . .

. . . no decent, right-minded, upstanding American citizen can for a moment countenance the shower of lying statements, with no basis in fact, that has been reduced to printed matter and sent broadcast through the mails of this country.

If the American people are willing to sit silently by and see large amounts of money secretly poured into false and misleading propaganda for political purposes, I repeat that I see in this not only a danger to the party but a danger to the country.

. . .

. . . the wicked motive of religious intolerance has driven bigots to attempt to inject these slanders into a political campaign. I here and now drag them into the open and I denounce them as a treasonable attack upon the very foundations of American liberty.

I have been told that politically it might be expedient for me to remain silent upon this subject, but so far as I am concerned no political expediency will keep me from speaking out in an endeavor to destroy these evil attacks.

There is abundant reason for believing that Republicans high in the councils of the party have countenanced a large part of this form of campaign if they have not actually promoted it. A sin of omission is sometimes as grievous as a sin of commission.

. . .

One of the things, if not the meanest thing in the campaign, is a circular pretending to place some one of my faith in the position of seeking votes for me because of my Catholicism. Like everything of its kind, of course, it is unsigned, and it would be impossible to trace its authorship. It reached me through a member of the Masonic order, who, in turn, received it in the mail. It is false in its every line. It was designed on its very face to injure me with members of churches other than my own.

I here emphatically declare that I do not wish any member of my faith in any part of the United States to vote for me on any religious grounds. I want them to vote for me only when in their hearts and consciences they become convinced that my election will promote the best interests of our country.

By the same token, I cannot refrain from saying that any person who votes against me simply because of my religion is not, to my way of thinking, a good citizen. Let me remind the Democrats of this country that we belong to the party of Thomas Jefferson, whose proudest boast was that he was the author of the Virginia statute for religious freedom. Let me remind the citizens of every political faith that that statute of religious freedom has become a part of the sacred heritage of our land.

There is pathos in one of Smith's closing paragraphs, so like the words he had used in his "Reply" to Charles Marshall:

The absolute separation of state and church is part of the fundamental basis of our Constitution. I believe in that separation and in all that it implies. That belief must be a part of the fundamental faith of every true American. Let the people of this country decide this election upon the great and real issues of the campaign, and upon nothing else.[53]

Smith's Oklahoma City address dominated the news. The New York *Herald Tribune*, which had attempted to destroy the effect of the speech before its delivery by imputing clever political motives, probed the one weak spot in an otherwise great effort. Governor Smith, said the *Herald Tribune*, would brand as bigots all who opposed him for whatever reason.[54] It is true and understandable that the Democratic candidate was sometimes disinclined to recognize sincerity in objections to his candidacy that were but distantly or not at all related to his religion. He charged that former Senator Owen was demagogic in his alarmist outcry about Tammany. The point, however plausible, could not be proved. In pushing his charge of insincerity, Smith strengthened the suspicion that he did not comprehend the emotional impact contained in the word "Tammany."

The Governor's opponents ridiculed his declaration that he did not want the votes of anyone on religious grounds. That Smith hoped to advance his election prospects through his Oklahoma City speech did not violate any ethical principle. He was the aggrieved party. His complete sincerity and feeling of outrage as a Catholic and as an American are patent. If he did not fully comprehend objections to his candidacy that would have been made—to a lesser degree—had he been a Protestant, that fact is an insignificant point in comparison with the effrontery, or partisan obtuseness, shown by those who blamed Smith for introducing the religious issue into the campaign. On this point the lead editorial in the New York *World*, entitled "The First Stone," told the truth:

Nicholas Longworth, Speaker of the House of Representatives, told a Republican audience in the Brooklyn Academy of Music on Monday evening that it was no fault of the Republican Party "if the religious issue has been thrown into this campaign." Ex-Gov. Henry J. Allen of Kansas told the same audience that Gov. Smith has "cast the first stone of religious intolerance in Oklahoma City." Neither of these statements, we believe, is true.

The Republican Party, certainly, cannot expect to shrug away responsibility for making use of the religious issue when the Republican National Committeeman of Alabama admits that he has distributed 250,000 copies of a circular attacking Gov. Smith's religion and when Mrs. Willebrandt appeals to the Methodist Church as a church to "swing the election" for Mr. Hoover and is thereupon honored by being placed upon the official list of speakers in the 1928 Campaign.

As for "casting the first stone," we ask Mr. Allen to remember that Gov. Smith did not organize the Ku Klux Klan, which has been traducing him for the last ten years. Gov. Smith did not organize the Methodist Board of Temperance, Prohibition and Public Morals, with its loose tongue and its unbridled bigotry. Gov. Smith did not organize the Anti-Saloon League of Ohio, which is now appealing to those who believe in "Anglo-Saxon Protestant domination" to defeat the Democratic ticket.* Gov. Smith did not organize the stories of his

* The *World's* short quotation from *The American Issue* is from the "Ohio Edition." The statement there printed is so clear a formulation of this widely held viewpoint, which greatly influenced the election, that further excerpts are given:

> Hoover and Smith are as opposite as the poles. They are types of directly opposite elements in our American life. Hoover represents the staid, reliable, dependable civilization which has built up America and maintained its high standards.
>
> Al Smith is a new type of Presidential candidate. Neither party has offered such a candidate for chief executive of the nation. This is said not because Smith is a Catholic, but because he is different from any candidate of either party within the knowledge of the present generation. He appeals to the sporty,

private life which have welled up in various backwoods sections of this country in dirty, shameless lies.[56]

Reports from many states and smaller localities do not show that the fires of bigotry burned less fiercely after Smith's speech at Oklahoma City. This, however, does not reduce the importance of that address. Rightly outraged by the campaign of misrepresentation, Smith imputed a single motive to opposition which was inspired by multiple causes. He felt sure that far beyond official admissions, his Catholic religion was a major part of the campaign against him and that it was often hidden beneath more reputable objections to his candidacy. Detailed on-the-spot press reports on opinion in various localities in Oklahoma, as in many other states, make it altogether clear that fear of the Roman Catholic church was a powerful reason for the drive to defeat him. At Oklahoma City, Smith neither invented nor introduced the issue. His address there stands beside his "Reply" to Marshall as a great effort in the arduous struggle to extend freedom in the United States.*

---

jazz, and liberal element of our population. He is not in harmony with the principles of our forefathers.

. . .

If you believe in Anglo-Saxon Protestant domination, if you believe in the maintenance of that civilization founded by our puritan ancestors, and preserved by our fathers; if you believe in those principles which have made this country what it is; if you believe in prohibition, its observance and enforcement, and if you believe in a further restricted immigration rather than letting down the bars still lower, then whether you are a Republican or a Democrat, you will vote for Hoover rather than Smith.[55]

* The forces of intolerance were more than a match for those who hoped to divert or stop the slander campaign in the brief

The day following Smith's speech was anticlimactic in Oklahoma City. The vocal forces of Righteousness had their day. Rev. John Roach Straton, who had been in Smith's audience the night before, was the imported celebrity. Straton retold the story of how he had "barred" the Governor from Calvary Baptist Church. He was in Oklahoma City to give assurance that Al Smith would never set foot in the White House. According to the *Daily Oklahoman* Straton's address marked him as a "master of the most caressing rhetoric."[58] With Straton was a local minister typical of those sensational evangelists who in booming voice proclaimed and defamed, Rev. Mordecai Fowler Ham.* With no regard for clear reports to the contrary from the local police department, Dr. Ham charged that the platform on which Smith pleaded for tolerance the night before had abounded with drunks.[60] It is regrettably true that there were others in the South and Southwest, and elsewhere in the nation, too, whose words and conduct in 1928 differed little from Dr. Ham's.

---

period from July to November, 1928. Among those organizations that tried to change the course, especially in the hectic last two months, none did more than the Calvert Associates. The Calverts were a group of Protestants and Catholics united for this end. Outstanding Protestants, one of them Dr. Ralph Adams Cram, the celebrated architect of the Episcopal Cathedral of St. John the Divine, worked in cooperation with such eminent Catholics as Michael Williams, editor of *Commonweal.* They wrote letters, ran newspaper advertisements depicting the nature of the attack on Smith's religion, and arranged for such champions of fair play as Dr. van Dyke to appeal on the radio.[57]

* It was reported to a *New York Times* correspondent by one who had been present that Dr. Ham had informed his congregation

Smith's speech in Oklahoma was answered by Mrs. Willebrandt in an address before a group of Methodist ministers in Ohio. She accused the Governor of "hiding behind his own church, because he is afraid to come out and face the record that he had made as a champion of the liquor traffic."[61] She correctly pointed out that it was Smith's telegram to the Houston convention that had made Prohibition a party issue. Hinting at a new approach which she developed at length a fortnight later, the Assistant Attorney General said that the Prohibition crusade was not an exclusively Protestant affair. She remarked that Catholics were among those who formed the army of the defenders of Prohibition.[62]

Mrs. Willebrandt, whom the scholarly Henry van Dyke referred to as "a female firebrand who is going through the Protestant churches kindling the flames of sectarian animosity,"[63] would have won few votes in a popularity contest* in the East. But there was an in-

---

that "If you vote for Al Smith, you're voting against Christ and you'll all be damned."[59]

* The writer has made a deliberate effort in this book to avoid the use of the ultrasensational or ultrasarcastic commentaries on leading figures in the campaign. However, in the case of Mrs. Willebrandt, the reaction was such that a sample of the hostile view of her activities, with some of its special quality, is justified by the need to let the reader glimpse the color of the campaign. The following, a special Washington report for the Houston *Post-Dispatch*, will serve this end:

> Putting it quite brutually, and in the parlance of Mrs. Willebrandt's prohibition enforcement cases, the assistant United States attorney general has the political goods on Dr. Work. With that the amiable physician of the Grand Old Party will not agree for publication. Yet there is plenty of material in the correspond-

sistent demand for more Willebrandt speeches. What, precisely, was her status? Did the Republican National Committee approve her speeches? Questioned about this, Chairman Work was exceedingly vague, but Representative Walter H. Newton, head of the Speakers' Bureau of the Republican National Committee, admitted that Mrs. Willebrandt's popularity topped all others and that her services were in great demand in "every part of the Middle West." Of course the high command of the Republican party was well aware that Mrs. Willebrandt's task was to help solidify the Protestant-Prohibitionist vote behind Hoover. There was much about Mrs. Willebrandt's activities that left a sour taste even with some of Mr. Hoover's supporters. In

---

ence files of the Republican Chicago headquarters, as well as in the files of the headquarters at Washington, to explain the hitherto inexplicable overnight about-face of the Republican national chairman, on the subject of the party's responsibility for Mrs. Willebrandt's speeches to the Methodists of Ohio.

Again borrowing a term from the lingo of the bootleggers and racketeers, Dr. Work "ran out" on Mrs. Willebrandt after her anti-Smith speech before the Ohio conference of Methodist Episcopal churches at Springfield, O., September 7. The Republican party, it was firmly indicated at national headquarters, was not responsible for that cry of "To your pulpits, O Parsons!" which started the Smith guns abanging on the religious issue.

The doctor got away with that.

But when he tried it again after Mrs. Willebrandt's speech at Lorain, O., before the Northeastern Ohio Methodist Episcopal conference, she called him hard, as they say in Texas.

Things began to happen right away. One day Dr. Work was saying that Mrs. Willebrandt was a free lance and that he was in no way responsible for her. The next day the Republican national committee publicly accepted full responsibility. Like Mr. Kipling's Yellow Dog Dingo, it had to. This is why—and it is susceptible to proof under subpoena duces tecum.[64]

view of this fact, perhaps it was to be expected that Chairman Work would respond vaguely to questions about the crusader from the Justice Department. A reporter from the *Herald Tribune*, who questioned Dr. Work about the status of Mrs. Willebrandt, got this reply:

"She's a Department of Justice official, you know that. She is a sort of free lance. Sometimes she goes out on her own and sometimes the committee sends her out."

"Do you approve of all of her speeches?" the chairman was asked.

"Those she has made or those she is to make?" Work inquired.

"Those she has made."

"I have not read them."

"You will find them interesting reading when you get around to them."

"That will have to be after the campaign," the chairman said, terminating the interview.[65]

Mrs. Willebrandt continued to hammer on the twin themes of Prohibition and Tammany Hall. She denounced the Hall and assured her audiences that Smith would ever be its true son. New York City was the "worst spot" in the United States, hardly a fit place from which to select a President. She denied the charge that, by appealing to sectarian, Protestant groups to vote for Hoover, she was guilty of injecting the religious issue into the campaign. Many felt that her denials had no substantive merit. The Republican administration, of which Mrs. Willebrandt was a part, brought fair criticism on itself when it made no voluntary move to meet the problem. It is not strange that when an official of the Republican administration's Justice Department talked primarily to Protestant groups that had long histories of anti-Catholic bias, the furies were loosed.

Mrs. Willebrandt was aware that the best defense is attack. Not long before, she had hinted at the nature of her new verbal weapon. At Owensboro, Kentucky, just four weeks before election day, she revealed it. Aiming to counteract the favorable reception that Smith's Oklahoma City speech had had in many quarters, she quoted part of a letter from the Louisville Catholic businessman and Democrat, Patrick H. Callahan. Not only was Colonel Callahan a strong dry but, as Mrs. Willebrandt was careful to tell her audience, he had been chairman of the Knights of Columbus Commission on Religious Prejudice when, a dozen years earlier, there had been a new wave of anti-Catholicism.[66] Callahan had been a strong Bryan and, later, McAdoo supporter and had vigorously opposed the nomination of a wet by the Democratic party. Mrs. Willebrandt told her Kentucky audience that Callahan could find nothing in her speeches "where you had any criticism whatever of the Catholic Church or refer to the religion of the Democratic candidate or his campaign manager." Callahan was sure that the Eighteenth Amendment*

> . . . was as important to the Methodists as the parochial school to the Catholics, and he could well imagine that if a Presidential candidate should attack the parochial schools it would be proper for a speaker before a Catholic conference to urge the defeat of such a candidate.[68]

* In her account of the events of 1928 Mrs. Willebrandt quotes from Callahan's letter. The quotations are substantially the same.[67]

Mrs. Willebrandt's final move, timed in a way reminiscent of the 1884 "Rum, Romanism and Rebellion" episode, came on the very eve of the election. She was talking in Los Angeles. According to the *Herald Tribune*, "Mrs. Willebrandt asserted that prohibition had its birth in Ireland in the middle of last century when Father Mathew, a Catholic priest, inspired the movement which culminated in the Eighteenth Amendment."

She described Lincoln and a number of recent popes as Prohibitionists and added, "To answer that these great leaders merely favored temperance in the use of alcohol and not total abstinence and the abolition of the whole liquor traffic is not only irreverent sophistry but treason to the Catholic Church."

Either the research that produced this great discovery must have been completed no earlier than the very eve of the election, or Mrs. Willebrandt stands self-accused of withholding very vital information from the American people. For these are her words:

> Until the last few years America has been free from intolerance and bigotry. And in this campaign nearly all of the bitterness, intolerance and bigotry of Democrats and Republicans alike could have been avoided if the truth about the Eighteenth Amendment had been known from the first.[69]

"The truth," of course, was Mrs. Willebrandt's revelation of the Catholic, as well as Protestant, roots of Prohibition. When all is said that can be said in support of this contention, when the work of the relatively few

Catholic leaders who favored Prohibition is taken into account, Mrs. Willebrandt's revelation remains a distortion of history and a last-minute effort to win votes among Catholics.*

* Certainly Mrs. Willebrandt's characterization of those who would distinguish between the temperance and Prohibition movements as guilty of "irreverent sophistry" ought to have made stanch Prohibitionists wince. But a campaign that was a crusade was under way, in fact so far under way that an effective political response to Mrs. Willebrandt's neat gymnastics was as impossible as it had proved to be in 1884, when Blaine was unable to offset the eleventh-hour damage done by the "Rum, Romanism and Rebellion" charge. There was not even sufficient time to apply to Mrs. Willebrandt's speech the descriptive term which Republicans used to describe Smith's Oklahoma City effort—a political trick. Election day was Tuesday, November 6. Mrs. Willebrandt got such headlines forty-eight hours before as, "Mrs. Willebrandt Praises Catholic Dry Act Loyalty . . . Tells Los Angeles Priest Inspired Eighteenth Amendment."[70]

Conclusion

The details of the events of the last few weeks of the campaign need not concern us here. The issue of Smith's Catholicism remained important until election day. The pattern of the campaign within a campaign was fixed long before Smith made his appeal in Oklahoma. For ten days after the Oklahoma City speech, according to the North American Newspaper Alliance, the religious issue led all others in newspaper space. Thereafter it returned increasingly to a covert status.

Smith lost the election by a wide margin, although he polled the largest popular vote any Democratic candidate had yet received. Doubtless the huge vote was chiefly due to those special issues that were symbolized by Al Smith. Unless much circumstantial evidence is meaningless, many cast their ballots more *against* Smith than *for* Hoover. The Upper South, together with Florida and Texas, voted Republican, thus breaking the tradition of the Solid South. A combination of factors, so interlaced as to defy complete separation, explain the defection of half the South. For the country as a whole, prosperity was the key issue. The religious factor is of particular importance both for 1928 and for the future course of American history. The concomitant social issues of great importance included Prohibition, the race question, immigration, snobbery, and a determination that the highest office in the land must not be held by someone thought to be alien to the American tradition.

After the defeat, all sorts of explanations were offered. There was jubilation among those who had opposed Smith, and there was bitterness and frustration among those who had backed him. The writer found in many letters a note of pathos. Some Catholics felt resentment and a deep sense of rejection. Some felt that a "second-class citizenship" status for Catholics was the lesson of Smith's defeat. This was altogether natural; it was expressed chiefly in the few days or weeks immediately after Hoover's sweeping victory.

The Catholic clergy, who had in most instances abstained from politics during this very trying period, were praised by fair-minded non-Catholics. Some Catholics professed to see a silver lining in Smith's defeat. This, of course, does not mean that there would have been a lack of satisfaction on their part had Smith become the first Catholic President, but there was an appreciation that a Catholic President would have experienced special difficulties in taking normal action in certain sectors of public policy.

Was there in operation in 1928 an "unwritten law" that barred a Catholic from the highest office in the land, an office which was peculiarly hedged about with an ultimate psychic as well as constitutional importance? Confused as the campaign was, the answer to this question, on the basis of the evidence, fortunately is in the negative. At no time did any responsible political

Alfred E. Smith and Franklin D. Roosevelt at Madison Square Garden, November 3, 1928. (Wide World Photo)

leader propose that the election be considered a formal mandate on the eligibility of a Catholic for the presidency. Had Smith again been nominated—as in early 1932 he hoped to be—and had he lost again in so auspicious a year, by however narrow a margin, a different answer might well be given. But Smith was denied the opportunity to run again. Since the Democratic debacle of 1924, which many blamed on the Smith forces, the star of another statesman who was unhampered by the fetters of a suspect religion and unembarrassed by social handicaps had risen rapidly. But had there been no Franklin D. Roosevelt, Smith might have fared no better in 1932. The search was on for a candidate who would not be "an offense to the villagers."

The belief in a Catholic taboo was in the minds of the politicians long before 1928. Obviously the taboo was not absolute, for Smith was nominated—a very notable event. But Smith's defeat furnished a point of reference which sharpened the presentiment that no Catholic could win. Since 1932 there have been prominent Catholics whose religion in all probability has been a handicap in the minds of politicians, whose business it is to win elections. In the years since 1932 there have been Catholics who, apart from their religion, would be considered possible nominees for the presidency or the vice-presidency. Some are today so considered. Their prospects are reduced by their religious affiliation. In the context of the present-day concern about Communism a Catholic nominee could be expected both to appeal to and, perhaps to a lesser degree, repel voters, because of his Church's well-known and uncompromising opposition to that undemocratic and unpopular "ism." Holdover arguments from 1928 and generations earlier would be revived, though other facts about the candidate would, of course, weigh heavily. Of course, Catholic statesmen, like others, have been handicapped in ways having no relationship to their religion. And there has been a plethora of available non-Catholic candidates.

Perhaps the next nomination of a Catholic will be for the vice-presidency rather than the presidency. When a member of the Catholic church first serves as Chief Executive, and when the country approves the result, perhaps then and then only will the Catholic taboo disappear. It will then be assumed that, despite differences in theory, all capable and loyal Methodist, Baptist, Unitarian, Jewish, Catholic, or agnostic candidates—all of whom are now qualified under the Constitution—should be considered equally eligible in a practical as well as legal sense for the presidency. When that time arrives, it will no longer be possible to conduct a campaign within a campaign employing the arguments used against Al Smith in 1928.

Until that moment it will be well to remember that, although the defeat of Smith was caused by a combination of forces and factors, his religion played a large, though not wholly calculable, part. A repetition of personalities and issues even remotely like the combination that existed in 1928 is impossible. Even with significant differences, however, there is no evidence that religious controversy has disappeared as a potentially divisive force in the political life of the United States.

References

Chapter One

1. Paul Leicester Ford (ed.), *The New-England Primer* (New York, 1897), 50.

2. Alfred E. Smith, *Up to Now, An Autobiography* (New York, 1929), 410–16.

3. See John Tracy Ellis, *The Life of James Cardinal Gibbons, Archbishop of Baltimore, 1834-1921* (Milwaukee, 1952), II: 1–80, on Americanism.

4. See J. Ryan Beiser, *The Vatican Council and The American Secular Newspapers, 1869-70* (Catholic University, Ph.D. Thesis, 1941), *passim.*

5. Theodore Maynard, *The Story of American Catholicism* (New York, 1951), 510.

6. *The Catholic Encyclopedia*, XIV: 537–38.

7. A condensed statement about the A.P.A., by the leading scholar, Humphrey J. Desmond, is in *The Catholic Encyclopedia*, I: 426–28.

8. Cardinal Gibbons, *North American Review*, CLXXXIX (March, 1909), 320–36.

9. Allan Nevins, *Grover Cleveland, A Study in Courage* (New York, 1933), 182.

10. Henry L. Stoddard, *As I Knew Them* (New York, 1927), 131.

11. Anson Phelps Stokes, *Church and State in the United States* (New York, 1950), II: 401–3.

12. *The Literary Digest*, XLII (June 17, 1911), 1203.

13. *Ibid.*, XXXIX (September 11, 1909), 386–87.

14. Stokes, *Church and State*, II: 400.

15. Ellis, *Gibbons*, II: 381.

16. Michael Williams, *The Shadow of the Pope* (New York and London, 1932), 115–16.

17. Washington Gladden, "The Anti-Papal Panic," *Harper's Weekly*, LIX (July 18, 1914), 55–56.

Chapter Two

1. From a sermon by Methodist Bishop Adna W. Leonard of Buffalo, N. Y., *The New York Times,* August 9, 1926.
2. John Moffatt Mecklin, *The Ku Klux Klan: A Study of the American Mind* (New York, 1924), 13–14. See also Williams, *The Shadow of the Pope,* 133.
3. C. Lewis Fowler, *The Ku Klux Klan—Its Origin, Meaning and Scope of Operation* (Atlanta, 1922), 19.
4. *The New York Times,* April 6, 1924.
5. *Ibid.*, April 7, 1924.
6. *America,* XXXI (April 26, 1924), 31.
7. *Forum,* LXXII (July, 1924), 76–83.
8. *Ibid.*, 78–79.
9. *Ibid.*, 80.
10. *Ibid.*, 26.
11. Roosevelt to Daniels, May 26, 1924, Daniels *Papers,* Library of Congress, Washington, D. C.
12. *The New York Times,* July 1, 1924.
13. Henry T. Rainey to Roosevelt, December 30, 1924, Roosevelt *Papers,* Franklin D. Roosevelt Library, Hyde Park, N. Y.
14. M. A. Potter to Roosevelt, December 13, 1924, Roosevelt *Papers.*
15. Herbert Hoover, *The Memoirs of Herbert Hoover, The Cabinet and the Presidency, 1920-1933* (New York, 1952), 201; also *The New York Times,* August 12, 1928.
16. *Forum,* LXXIII (March, 1925), 289.
17. *Ibid.*, 289–301.
18. *Ibid.*, LXXIV (July, 1925), 72–74.
19. *Ibid.*, (August, 1925), 300–301.
20. The *World,* New York, June 17, 1926.
21. *Kourier Magazine,* II (September, 1926), 19–20.
22. *The Personal Papers of Alfred E. Smith,* New York State Library, Albany, N. Y.
23. *The New York Times,* August 9, 1926.
24. *Ibid.*, August 20, 1926.
25. *Ibid.*, August 9, 1926.
26. *Wesleyan University Alumnus,* XI (October, 1926), 69; cf. *The New York Times,* September 24, 1926.
27. *America,* XXXV (August 21, 1926), 438.
28. *The New York Times,* August 10, 1926.
29. The *World,* New York, August 9, 1926.
30. *Ibid.*, August 10, 1926.

31. *Ibid.*
32. *The New York Times,* August 11, 1926.
33. *Ibid.,* August 13, 1926.
34. *Ibid.*
35. The *World,* New York, August 13, 1926.
36. *The New York Times,* December 3, 1926.
37. *Ibid.,* December 8, 1926.
38. *Ibid.,* October 5, 1926.
39. *Ibid.,* October 7, 1926.
40. *Ibid.,* October 10, 1926.
41. *Ibid.,* December 28, 1926.
42. *Ibid.,* December 14, 1926.
43. *Outlook,* CXLIV (December 15, 1926); see also *The New York Times,* December 11, 1926.
44. *The New York Times,* August 1, 1926.
45. *America,* XXXV (August 14, 1926), 415.

Chapter Three

1. Alfred E. Smith, *Atlantic Monthly,* CXXXIX (May, 1927), 728.
2. *America,* XXXVII (May 7, 1927), 78.
3. *Christian Register,* CVI (January 6, 1927), 2.
4. *Ibid.,* 3.
5. *The New York Times,* January 2, 1927.
6. *Christian Register,* CVI (January 20, 1927), 45–48.
7. *America,* XXXVI (February 5, 1927), 404–6.
8. *Atlantic Monthly,* CXXXIX (April, 1927), 540–49.
9. *Ibid.* (May, 1927), 721–28.
10. Lithgow Osborne to Roosevelt, January 28, 1927, Roosevelt *Papers.*
11. Roosevelt to Osborne, February 2, 1927, *ibid.*
12. Ellery Sedgwick, *Atlantic Harvest* (Boston, 1947), xxi–xxiii.
13. Donald B. Snyder, of the *Atlantic,* to the writer, July 29, 1955.
14. Conversation with Mr. Sedgwick, September 8, 1952, and a letter from Mr. Sedgwick to the writer, September 21, 1952.
15. *America,* XL (October 27, 1928), 54.
16. *Atlantic Monthly,* CXXXIX (April, 1927), 541.
17. Sedgwick to Roosevelt, March 3, 1927, Roosevelt *Papers.*
18. Sedgwick to Mrs. Nelson Sale, October 25, 1928, Sedgwick file in the writer's possession.

19. Roosevelt (at Warm Springs, Ga.) to Smith, March 10, 1927, Roosevelt *Papers.*
20. Roosevelt to Sedgwick, March 19, 1927, Roosevelt *Papers.*
21. Conversation with Mr. Sedgwick, September 8, 1952.
22. Sedgwick, *Atlantic Harvest*, xxiii.
23. *Atlantic Monthly*, CXXXIX (May, 1927), 728.
24. *Ibid.*, CXL (July, 1927), 140.

Chapter Four

1. George Fort Milton to Walsh, January 28, 1928, Walsh *Papers.*
2. *Catholic World*, CXXVIII (October, 1928), 102.
3. U. S. *Congressional Record*, 70th Cong., 1st Sess., January 18, 1928, Vol. 69, Part 2, 1661.
4. *Ibid.*, January 23, 1928, 1866.
5. *Ibid.*, January 18, 1928, 1654–55.
6. *Ibid.*
7. *Ibid.*, May 17, 1928, Part 8, 8941–42.
8. *Commonweal*, V (February 9, 1927), 372–75.
9. *The New York Times*, January 2, 1928.
10. *New Republic*, LV (July 4, 1928), 175.
11. Mr. and Mrs. H. M. Morrissette to Daniels, March 22, 1924, Daniels *Papers.*
12. Daniels to Mr. and Mrs. H. M. Morrissette, April 1, 1924, *ibid.*
13. Daniels to J. D. Taylor, April 19, 1927, *ibid.*
14. The Reverend G. L. Kerr of the Associate Reformed Presbyterian Church, Spartanburg, S. C., to Daniels, April 14, 1927, *ibid.*
15. J. S. Garvin to Daniels (no date, but Daniels' reply refers to date as May 2, 1927), *ibid.*
16. C. H. Kimball to Daniels, April 12, 1927, *ibid.*
17. Mimeo. letter, Callahan to Senator Glass, April 28, 1927, Callahan *Correspondence.*
18. Billington, *Protestant Crusade*, 99–108.
19. *Commonweal*, V (March 30, 1927), 562; *New Republic*, L (March 23, 1927), 128–31.
20. Quoted in Callahan to Walsh, March 26, 1928, Walsh *Papers.*
21. The Reverend Stanley G. Tyndall of the Independent Church of the Covenant, Brooklyn, N. Y., to Walsh, March 21, 1926, *ibid.*

22. Walsh to Tyndall, March 22, 1926, *ibid.*
23. John W. Bennett to Daniels, April 9, 1927, Daniels *Papers.*
24. Sullivan to Milton, February 27, 1928, attached to Milton to Walsh, March 1, 1928, Walsh *Papers.*
25. J. T. Carroll to Walsh, May 2, 1928, *ibid.*
26. Mary F. Casey to Walsh, March 3, 1928, *ibid.*
27. Mrs. G. E. Thomas to Walsh, March 6, 1928, *ibid.*
28. Walsh to Mary F. Casey, March 7, 1928, *ibid.*
29. Walsh to Mrs. G. E. Thomas, March 19, 1928, *ibid.*
30. C. S. Mann to Callahan, January 5, 1929, Callahan *Correspondence.*
31. Walsh to J. F. T. O'Connor, January 24, 1929, Walsh *Papers.*
32. Clinton C. Stevens to Daniel C. Roper, March 22, 1928, *ibid.*
33. *Forum,* LXXIX (June, 1928), 809–25; *Christian Century,* XLV (June 14, 1928), 751–52.
34. *Commonweal,* VIII (June 6, 1928), 123–24.

Chapter Five

1. New York *Herald Tribune,* July 15, 1928. AP dispatch.
2. See any of the "Americana" columns in *The American Mercury* of this period.
3. *The New York Times,* April 4, 1927.
4. *Ibid.,* June 30, 1928.
5. Glass to Mrs. W. R. Pattangall, Augusta, Me., September 5, 1928, Senator Carter Glass *Papers,* University of Virginia, Charlottesville, Va.
6. Milton to McAdoo, July 31, 1928, Senator Furnifold McLendel Simmons *Papers,* Duke University Library, Durham, N. C.
7. Morris Robert Werner, *Tammany Hall* (Garden City, N. Y., 1928).
8. New York *Herald Tribune,* April 22, 1928.
9. *The New York Times,* July 12, 1928.
10. *Ibid.,* June 27, 1928.
11. *Ibid.,* July 15, 1928.
12. Roosevelt to Daniels (with envelope marked "for the safe"), July 20, 1928, Daniels *Papers.*
13. *The New York Times,* July 25, 1928.
14. *Ibid.,* April 11, 1928.
15. Smith, *Autobiography,* 410–12.
16. Hoover, *Memoirs,* 205–9.

17. *Collier's Weekly*, LXXVIII (August 21, 1926), 8, 9.
18. New York *Herald Tribune*, August 1, 1928.
19. *Ibid.*, July 15, 1928. AP dispatch.
20. *Ibid.*
21. *Ibid.*
22. *Ibid.*
23. Walter Johnson, *William Allen White's America* (New York, 1947), 408.
24. New York *Herald Tribune*, July 29, 1928.
25. *Ibid.*, July 31, 1928.
26. Johnson, *White's America*, 409.
27. *The New York Times*, August 1, 1928.
28. New York *Herald Tribune*, August 2, 1928.
29. Johnson, *White's America*, 410.
30. New York *Herald Tribune*, August 15, 1928.
31. *The New York Times*, August 4, 1928.
32. *World's Work*, LVI (September, 1928), 485.
33. New York *Herald Tribune*, feature article, August 12, 1928.
34. *Ibid.*, August 6, 1928.
35. *Ibid.*
36. *Ibid.*, August 8, 1928.
37. *Ibid.*, August 9, 1928.
38. *Ibid.*, August 10, 1928.
39. *Ibid.*
40. *Ibid.*, August 13, 1928.
41. *Ibid.*, August 15, 1928.
42. *Ibid.*
43. *Ibid.*, August 18, 1928.
44. *Ibid.*, August 10, 1928.
45. *The New York Times*, August 6, 1928.
46. New York *Herald Tribune*, August 27, 1928.

Chapter Six

1. Reinhold Niebuhr, *Commonweal*, LVIII (May 8, 1953), 117–20.
2. Morton Harrison, *Atlantic Monthly*, CXLI (May, 1928), 680.
3. *Ibid.*, 686.
4. See Robert Coughlin, "Konklave in Kokomo," *The Aspirin Age*, Isabel Leighton (ed.), (New York, 1949), 105–29.
5. *The New York Times*, September 29, 1928.
6. *Ibid.*

7. *Ibid.*

8. *Ibid.*, September 30, 1928.

9. Washington *Post*, September 30, 1928.

10. Hoover, *Memoirs*, 205, 207.

11. *Ibid.*, 208, 209.

12. New York *Herald Tribune*, September 1, 1928.

13. *Ibid.*, September 4, 1928.

14. U. S., *Congressional Record*, 62d Cong., 3d Sess., February 15, 1913, Vol. 49, Part 4, 3216.

15. Smith *Papers.*

16. The *World*, New York, October 3, 1928.

17. *The New York Times*, October 4, 1928.

18. Roy C. Frank, Solicitor, Post Office Department, Washington, D.C., December 4, 1952, and April, 1956, to the writer.

19. The *World*, New York, September 9, 1928.

20. "Governor Smith's Membership in the Roman Catholic Church and its Proper Place as an Issue in this Campaign," by Oliver D. Street, published by the Republican State Campaign Committee, Birmingham, Ala., Smith *Papers.*

21. The *World*, New York, October 2, 1928.

22. Simmons to E. M. Spivey, August 22, 1928, Simmons *Papers.*

23. The Houston *Chronicle*, September 28, 1928.

24. *The New York Times*, July 24, 1928.

25. F. O. Ticknor to the Monroe, N. C., *Journal*, August 2, 1928, Simmons *Papers.*

26. E. N. Freeman to Norris, October 28, 1928, *Personal Papers* of Senator George Norris, Library of Congress, Washington, D.C.

27. Robert H. Toot to Norris, October 26, 1928, Norris *Papers.*

28. Samuel H. Wiley to Simmons, August 8, 1929, Simmons *Papers.*

29. Rembert Gilman Smith, *Politics in a Protestant Church* (Atlanta, 1930), 70.

30. *Ibid.*, 71.

31. *Ibid.*

32. The *World*, New York, August 7, 1928.

33. New York *Herald Tribune*, September 10, 1928.

34. The *World*, New York, October 3, 1928.

35. Overman to A. M. Stack, September 22, 1928, Senator Lee S. Overman *Papers*, University of North Carolina Library, Chapel Hill.

36. *Ibid.*

37. C. F. Kirksey to Simmons, August 31, 1928, Simmons *Papers.*

38. Richard L. Watson, Jr. (ed.), *Bishop Cannon's Own Story* (Durham, N. C., 1955), xvii.
39. *Ibid.*, 399 and chap. x.
40. *The Voice*, XVI (August, 1928), 1.
41. *The New York Times*, July 20, 1928.
42. Watson, *Bishop Cannon*, 440.
43. *The Voice*, XVI (August, 1928), 2–3.
44. The *World*, New York, September 13, 1928.
45. New York *Herald Tribune*, September 2, 1928.
46. *The New York Times*, September 22, 1928.
47. *Catholic Telegraph*, XCVII (September 13, 1928), 1.
48. *The New York Times*, August 2, 1928.
49. *Ibid.*, August 8, 1928.
50. *Ibid.*, September 8, 1928.
51. New York *Herald Tribune*, September 8, 1928.
52. *Scrapbook, 1928*, Vol. 18, Kilroe Collection, Columbia University Library, New York.
53. New York *Herald Tribune*, September 21, 1928.
54. *Ibid.*
55. Typed copy from *The American Issue*, "Ohio Edition," (September 21, 1928), 3.
56. The *World*, New York, October 4, 1928.
57. J. M. Stuart, "The New Minute Men," *Commonweal*, VIII (October 3, 1928), 538–39.
58. *Daily Oklahoman*, Oklahoma City, September 22, 1928.
59. *The New York Times*, October 3, 1928.
60. *Daily Oklahoman*, September 22, 1928.
61. *The New York Times*, September 24, 1928.
62. *Ibid.*
63. *Ibid.*, October 4, 1928.
64. Houston *Post-Dispatch*, October 9, 1928.
65. New York *Herald Tribune*, September 26, 1928.
66. *Ibid.*, October 9, 1928.
67. Mabel Willebrandt, *The Inside of Prohibition* (Indianapolis, 1929), 333.
68. New York *Herald Tribune*, October 9, 1928.
69. *Ibid.*, November 4, 1928.
70. *Ibid.*

Bibliographical Note

No attempt is here made to give the reader a complete bibliography. Items used sparingly are omitted altogether, and attention is drawn only to books which would be particularly helpful to those who might wish to read further. In addition, items which have supplied the primary basis for the book are listed, even though they are not readily available to most readers.

The sources for this book are chiefly unprinted correspondence, lay and secular periodicals, newspapers, visual aids such as cartoons, and conversations with people who were active in politics at the time. Interviews have been helpful principally for background, for a fuller appreciation of the imponderables, and for a better understanding of a topic which the author has not discussed in the formal part of the book, namely, the Catholic question in presidential politics since Smith's defeat. Where the names of those interviewed enter the book, reliance has usually been placed on printed or unprinted sources rather than on interviews.

The most useful primary sources are the letters of politicians, journalists, and others who were prominent in the political life of the twenties, but some of the most revealing material consists of letters written to them by people of less prominence. Manuscripts are, of course, not complete for so recent a decade as the twenties, but what is available is sufficiently great in quantity to make selection necessary. In general, the focal point of this book is the Upper South and the Northeast, with lesser attention to other areas. Most important were the Norris *Papers*, the Thomas J. Walsh *Papers*, and the Josephus Daniels *Papers*, all at the Library of Congress; the Glass *Papers* at the University of Virginia; the Simmons *Papers* at Duke

University; the Overman *Papers* at the University of North Carolina; the Franklin D. Roosevelt *Papers* at the Franklin D. Roosevelt Library at Hyde Park; and the *Public and Private Papers* of Governor Smith at Albany. Unfortunately, the Smith *Papers* are not helpful on the subject of Smith's own attitudes since they contain no letters signed by him. Students of Smith's life are uniformly disappointed by the dearth of available material.

Catholic, Protestant, and secular periodicals are important sources. For liberal Protestant opinion the *Christian Century* is especially valuable; for an expression of Catholic views the diocesan papers are helpful, although they tend to run to a pattern. More useful are the files of *America* and of *Commonweal.* On the Protestant side there is a bewildering array of ephemeral periodicals in addition to the more important papers that are available in seminary and some other libraries. So far as is known, the many hundreds, and probably thousands, of short-lived local Protestant papers have never been brought together even in a catalogue. The *Christian Register* was particularly helpful for its poll of Protestant opinion on a Catholic President.

Much of the most revealing type of source is difficult to come upon because of its often disreputable character. This in part explains its wholesale destruction. Some of the low-level propaganda found its way into some of the manuscript collections listed above. The largest group of anti-Catholic illustrative material—cartoons, broadsides, front covers of scurrilous periodicals, etc.—is in the files of the *Private Papers* of Governor Smith (see also below under Michael Williams, *Shadow of the Pope*).

Newspapers from all sections were sampled, but concentrated use of this very important source was made in a number of papers published in the Upper South and in New York. Josephus Daniels' *News and Observer* (Raleigh, N. C.) was used consistently along with the Daniels *Papers.* Three New York City dailies were followed in detail—*The New York Times* which was pro-Smith, the *Herald Tribune* which supported Hoover, and the *World.* The last named was a particularly brilliant pro-Smith newspaper, very revealing for its cartoons (by Rollin Kirby), its outspoken editorials, and for its unusually full reports on the campaign in the South.

Though for so recent a decade authoritative historical works are yet unwritten, the following books are especially helpful for this volume, for its background or, in a few instances, on aspects of the theme after 1928.

Campaign Addresses of Governor Alfred E. Smith (Albany, 1929) should be supplemented by sometimes more revealing newspaper reports of the speeches. Edgar Eugene Robinson, *The Presidential Vote, 1896–1932* (Palo Alto, 1934), gives the presidential votes by counties as well as states. A brief and largely economic-political account of the Hoover-Smith election is Roy V. Peel and Thomas C. Donnelly, *The 1928 Campaign, An Analysis* (New York, 1931). Anson Phelps Stokes, *Church and State in the United States*, 3 vols. (New York, 1950), is an invaluable introduction by an Episcopalian scholar to many of the ramifications of this important and sensitive problem. Ray Allen Billington, *The Protestant Crusade, 1800–1860* (New York, 1952), is the classic work on the problem up to the Civil War. John Tracy Ellis, *The Life of James Cardinal Gibbons, Archbishop of Baltimore, 1834–1921* (Milwaukee, 1952), embodies much of the needed background in the four decades that centered on 1900. C. Vann Woodward, *Tom Watson, Agrarian Rebel* (New York, 1938), has revealing chapters on anti-Semitism and anti-Catholicism in Georgia before 1920.

The Smith material is very inadequate, but for a broad approach see Henry F. Pringle, *Alfred E. Smith, A Critical Study* (New York, 1927). *Up to Now, An Autobiography* (New York, 1929), by Alfred E. Smith, is disappointing but useful because of the scarcity of other Smith materials. Norman Hapgood and Henry Moskowitz, *Up From the City Streets* (New York, 1927), is a campaign document of interest. Parts of *The Memoirs of Herbert Hoover, The Cabinet and the Presidency, 1920–1933* (New York, 1952), are pertinent to the special issues of the election of 1928. Walter Johnson, *William Allen White's America* (New York, 1947), can be used profitably.

Two books by the editor of *Commonweal,* Michael Williams, are especially important because of their author's prominence in the effort to curb bigotry. These are *Catholicism and the Modern Mind* (New York, 1928) and *The Shadow of the Pope* (New York and London, 1932). The latter is usefully illustrated with pamphlet covers and other examples of anti-Catholic propaganda used in 1928.

Charles C. Marshall, *The Roman Catholic Church in the Modern State* (New York, 1928), supplies background for the views of its author and a large body of educated non-Catholics who feared a Catholic President. More insight into the high-level opposition can be found in Winfred Ernest Garrison, *Catholicism and the American Mind* (Chicago and New York, 1928).

On the part played by Methodist Bishop Cannon, see Virginius Dabney, *Dry Messiah, The Life of Bishop Cannon* (New York, 1949) and Richard L. Watson, Jr. (ed.), *Bishop Cannon's Own Story* (Durham, 1955).

For a brief but excellent summary of the economic and social patterns that affected the voting in 1928 in the South see V. O. Key, Jr., *Southern Politics in State and Nation* (New York, 1949).

James A. Farley, *Jim Farley's Story, The Roosevelt Years* (New York, 1948), gives a sidelight on the part Catholicism played in the 1940 election.

The reader interested in the subject's most contemporary relevance should consult the brief article by John J. Kane in *Commonweal* (February 17, 1956).

Index

Allen, Henry J., 134, 186
America
  editor's reaction to *Christian Register's* poll, 65
  on Caraway, 55
  "More Rum, Romanism and Rebellion," article on, 49
  religion as qualification for political office, article on, 58-59
American Catholicism, 18-19
American Inquisitors, 107
Americanism, 6-11, 18-19
American Issue, The, 186
American Protective Association, 9, 13, 15
"America's Two Unwritten Laws," 29
Anglo-Saxon civilization, 24, 163, 186, 187
  Leonard on, 48, 49
Anti-Saloon League, 47, 129
Anti-Semitism, 24, 27
A.P.A., see American Protective Association
Asheville Conference, 169-70
Atlantic Monthly, 60, 66, 67, 68; *see also* Marshall's "Letter"; Sedgwick, Ellery; Smith's "Reply"
Awful Disclosures, 90

Baptists, 45, 64, 165, 169-70, 188
Barton, A. J., 169-70
"Bible belt," 107, 108
Billington, Ray Allen, 4
Blaine, James G., 11-13, 179
Blakely, Paul L., 29-30
Board of Temperance, Prohibition and Public Morals, 51, 170-72, 186
Bonzano, Giovanni, 44, 45, 47
Boobus americanus, 107-108
Borah, William E., 176
Boston *Post*, 74, 75
Breckenridge, Henry, 53
Bruce, William C., 51
Bryan, William Jennings, 99, 107, 111, 120, 192
Burchard, Samuel D., 12
Butler, Nicholas Murray, 180

Cahensly, Peter, 5
Cahenslyism, 5-6
Caldwell, Mrs. Willie W., 146-47, 156
Callahan, P. H., 17, 90, 192
Calvary Baptist Church, 136, 137, 138, 140-41
Calvert Associates, 188
Campaigns, presidential
  1884, 11-13, 179
  1908, 13
  1924, 83
  1932, 150
"Can a Catholic be President?" article, 30
Candler, Warren A., 164-65
Cannon, James, Jr., 164, 169-70
Caraway, T. H., 54-55
Cardozo, B. N., 159
Carroll, J. T., 96
Carroll, John, 3
Catholic church, 162
  Americanism issue in, 6-11, 18-19
  clergy of, abstains from politics in 1928, 196
  Heflin's attacks on, 82
  members of ,"second-class citizenship," 196
  racial issue, 27, 157
Catholic Encyclopedia, 6, 8-9

Catholic News, 52
Catholic World, The, 81
Catholic party
  Heflin on, 83
  Munro on, 101-102
  Williams on, 101
Chattanooga *News*, 54
Christian Century, on Catholic party, 102
Christian Leader, 64-65
Christian Register
  discussion of dual allegiance, 60-62
  poll of Protestant editors on dual allegiance, 62-65
Church and state relations, 50, 73, 153, 168
  cartoon, 25
  Dieffenbach on, 60
  Duffy on, 62
  Freethinkers Society on, 44
  Gibbons' attitude toward, 7, 10
  Ireland's attitude toward, 7
  Leonard on, 48
  Wishart on, 61
Church and State in the United States, 18
Cleveland, Grover, 11-13, 22, 89, 120
Coffin, Henry Sloane, 52
Collier's Weekly, 129
Commission on Religious Prejudices, 17, 192
Commonweal, 42, 101, 188
  on Heflin, 85
  finds *New Republic* anti-Catholic, 91
Communism, 43, 199-200
Conboy, Martin, 30
Congressional Record, 82, 86, 153, 154
Conventions, Democratic
  1920, 22
  1924, 2, 32-35
    balloting deadlock, 32
    choice of site, 28
    fight over Klan, 32
    McAdoo's role in, 32-35
    nomination of Davis, 34
    Walsh's chairing, 93
    White on, 129
  1928
    Robinson's nomination, 110
    Smith's nomination, 2, 103-105, 112
    Smith's wet telegram, 113-14
Coolidge, Calvin, 32, 48, 120, 121, 175
Covenanters, 15-16
Cram, Ralph Adams, 188

Dabney, R. H.
  Forum article, 43-44
  New York Times letter, 53
Daily Oklahoman, 188
Daniels, Josephus
  letters to
    concerning Smith's candidacy, 88-90
    regarding Walsh's religion, 95
  on McAdoo's religion, 86
  1924 platform suggestion, 31
  Papers of, 86
  on religion as qualification for presidency, 87
  on Wilson and Pope, 87
Darrow, Clarence, 107
Davis, Elmer, on William Allen White, 135
Davis, John W., 34, 83, 111, 120
  Heflin on, 83
Dayton, Tennessee, 107
Democratic National Committee Chairman; *see* Raskob, John J.
Democratic party
  ascendency of Smith forces in 1928, 94
  conservative platform and campaign in 1928, 120
  1928 headquarters, 125
  Heflin on post-1924 demoralization of, 83
  nomination of Catholic, 2
  Smith denied 1932 nomination by, 199
  solid South, 112, 113

southern leaders oppose Smith's nomination, 58
wet telegram, reaction to, 113-14
Denny, Collins, 164
Dieffenbach, Albert C., 60-62
Dodge, Homer Joseph, 31
Dual allegiance, 59, 60-65, 68, 79; *see also* Marshall's "Letter"
DuBose, Horace M., 164
du Pont, Pierre S., 122
du Pont de Nemours, E. I., Co., 122
Duffy, Francis P., 61, 73, 156
on European church-state relationship, 62

E. A., 29, 173
Eighteenth Amendment, 163, 175-76, 192; *see also* Prohibition
Election results for 1928, 120, 195
Ellis, John Tracy, 18
Era of Progressivism, 21
Eucharistic Congress, Chicago, 44-45, 47, 55, 59, 61, 68, 156

Farm problem, 119
Fellowship Forum, The, 154
cartoons from, 25, 46, 109, 161
"First Stone, The," New York *World* editorial, 185-87
Fitzpatrick, D. R., cartoon, 177
Florida Cracker, 153
Ford, Henry, 2, 118
Forum, 30, 31, 43
on Catholic party, 102
Frank, Roy C., 154
Freethinkers Society, 44
Friars' land dispute, 13
Frost, Stanley, 101
Fundamentalism, 23, 24, 107, 118
Straton as leader of, 136-37

General Motors, 121-22
Gerard, James W., 182
Gibbons, James, 23, 42, 75
Americanism, 7-11
biography of, 18
on Cahenslyism, 6
church and state, 7, 10
opposed suppression of the *Menace*, 15
public schools, 75
testimonial meeting, 14
Gildersleeve, Virginia, 180
Glass, Carter, 113, 147
Griswold, Mrs. Florence T., 158
Guardians of Liberty, 15-16, 18
Guinan, Texas, 108

Ham, Mordecai Fowler, 188-89
"Happy Warrior"; *see* Smith, Alfred E.
Harding administration, 32-33, 96
Hecker, Isaac, 18
Heflin, Thomas J., 155
appeal to prejudice, 85
on Catholic party, 83
Commonweal on, 85
on Davis' defeat, 83
on Mexican issue, 82
New Republic on, 86
New York Times on, 85
on Raskob, 174-75
Robinson on, 82
"tar and feather" speech, 82
Herter, Christian, 66
Hicks, J. E., 165
Higham, John, 4
Hooded Order, see Ku Klux Klan
Hoover, Herbert, 119, 120, 142, 156, 157, 162
acceptance speech, 125, 150
on bigotry, 150-51, 156
Caldwell letter, repudiation by, 146
Memoirs of, 128, 149, 150
on Oklahoma City speech, 151
on Prohibition, 42
on religion as factor in election, 151-52
on religious tolerance, 150
on slander campaign, 128
on Smith's defeat, 151-52
on whispering campaign, 149
Hoover's *Memoirs*, 128, 149, 150
Houston *Chronicle*, 158
Houston *Post-Dispatch*, 189-90
Hughes, Charles Evans, 180

Independent, 66
Ireland, John, 23, 42
  Americanism, 7-9
  public schools, 75
  T. R. Roosevelt's admiration for, 14

Kirby, Rollin, cartoons, 139, 167
Kourier Magazine, 45, 59
Knights of Columbus, 27
  Commission on Religious Prejudices, 17, 192
  "oath," 91, 105, 153-54
Knights of Luther, 15-16
Know Nothingism, 4, 9, 13, 47
Ku Klux Klan, 44, 83, 100, 145, 163, 180, 186
  anti-Catholicism in South, 27
  anti-Semitism in South, 27
  background of, 23-28
  in 1928 campaign, 108, 110
  Catholic church's antisegregation stand, 27
  Democratic party, 1924, 27-28
  Eucharistic Congress, 47
  Knights of Columbus, 27
  Kourier Magazine, 45
  methods of, 27
  prevalence of, 24, 27
  Rainey on, 36
  Republican party, 27-28
  F. D. Roosevelt on, 72
  Smith, 23, 28, 110
  Tammany, 27, 50
  white supremacy, 24

La Follette, Robert, 20, 99, 146
  1924 candidacy of, 32, 34
Lansing, Robert, 180
Leo XIII, 5, 7, 8
Leonard, Adna W., 21
  attacks Smith, 47-51
Life of James Cardinal Gibbons, 18
Lincoln, Abraham, 193
Lippmann, Walter, 107
  and White, 133-34
Long, Breckenridge, 173
Longworth, Nicholas, 186
Lutherans, 170, 173
Lyon, Mrs. Clara R., 146

McAdoo, William Gibbs, 96, 110, 114, 192
  church affiliation, 86
  convention, 1924 Democratic, 32-35
  pre-1928 political inactivity, 38
McConaughy, James L., 48
McDaniel, George W., 45
McFaul, James A., 14-15
McKinley, William, 9
Madison Square Garden, 138; *see also* Convention, 1924 Democratic
Mann, C. S., 98
Mann, H. A., 155
Marshall, Charles C., 60, 66, 93, 103, 136; *see also* Marshall's "Letter"
Marshall's "Letter," 41, 44, 60, 66-79, 87, 93, 155, 156, 171
  F. D. Roosevelt on, 72
Masks in a Pageant, 130
Maynard, Theodore
  on Hecker, 18
  on *Testem Benevolentiae*, 18-19
Menace, 15
Mencken, Henry L., 107
"Methodist Pope, A," *New York Times* editorial, 49
Methodists, 47-51, 64, 163-65, 166, 169-70, 174, 176, 178, 186, 189, 190, 192
Mexican issue, 16-17, 63, 69, 89, 91
  Heflin on, 82
Miller, O. R., 129, 132
Milton, George Fort
  on campaign issue, 54
  on Heflin, 81
  on Smith's nomination, 114
Monk, Maria, 90
Moore, John M., 164
"More Rum, Romanism and Rebellion," article in *America*, 49
Moskowitz, Mrs. Belle, 67, 73, 159
Mouzon, Edwin D., 163-64
Munro, William Bennett, 101-102

National Crusader, The, 158
National Lutheran Editors' Association, 173

New-England Primer, The, 1
New Menace, The, 154
New Republic
  Commonweal finds, anti-Catholic, 91
  Heflin "Obituary," 86
Newton, Walter H., 190
New York *Herald Tribune,* 130, 191, 193
  Oklahoma City speech, 185
  reaction to Smith's "Reply," 76
  on Smith's use of religious issue, 179
  on Straton affair, 141-42
New York Times, The, 29, 52, 61, 85, 174, 188
  on bigotry, editorial, 148
  on 1924 Democratic convention, editorial, "Wicked Hospitality," 34-35
  letters to, 50, 51, 62, 135
  on Leonard, editorial, "A Methodist Pope," 49
  on Smith's nomination and Solid South, 110
  reaction to Smith's "Reply," 76
New York *World,* 85
  cartoon from, 167
  reports on Leonard, 49-50
  religion in campaign, editorial, "The First Stone," 185-87
  on Straton affair, 141, 142
Nicholson, Meredith, 58-59
Niebuhr, Reinhold, 145
"Noble experiment," 42; *see also* Prohibition
"No-Popery," 9, 13, 16, 88, 166
Norris, George, 58
North American Newspaper Alliance, 195

"Oath" of Knights of Columbus, 91, 105, 153-54
Oklahoma City speech; *see* Smith, Alfred E.
Overman, Lee S., on bigotry in campaign, 166
Owen, Robert L., 180, 182, 185

Papal Infallibility, Proclamation of Dogma of, 5
Parochial schools, 44, 192
  Smith on, 76
Parsons, Wilfred, 65
"Phantom heresy," 6
Payne, John Barton, 98
Pickett, Deets, 171-73
Pius IX, 4
Pius XI, 125
Post Office Department, U. S., 15, 154
Presbyterians, 52, 170, 173
Presbyterian Magazine, 173
Presidential Vote, 1896-1932, The, 120
Prohibition, 64, 162-63, 166, 175, 194; *see also* Eighteenth Amendment
  Democratic platform on, 113
  as focus of attacks on Smith, 39
  Henry Ford on, 2, 118
  "Noble experiment," 42
  parties split by, 2
  relationship to religious issue, 40, 117
  Smith's stand on, 22, 39, 131
  southern Protestants' stand on, 39
  Volstead Act, 22, 39
Prohibitionists, 16
Proskauer, Joseph M., 73, 159, 172
Protestant churches
  in 1928 campaign, 162-63, 165, 168, 178
  and Prohibition, 118
  replies to *Christian Register's* dual allegiance questions, 63-65
Protestant Crusade, The, 4
Public schools, 44
  cartoon, 25
  Gibbons, 8, 75
  Ireland, 8, 75
  Marshall on, 69
  Smith's record
    Robinson on, 152
    F. D. Roosevelt on, 73
    Smith on, 76
  Wishart, 61

Quakers
Hoover's religion as campaign issue, 150

Racial issue, 24-28, 157-58
Rainey, Henry T., 36
Raskob, John J.
background, 121-22
religion, 125-26
F. D. Roosevelt on, 122, 125
on southern Methodists, 173-74
Reformed Church Messenger, 63-64
Religious issue, 23-31, 39-55, 200
Republican National Committee, 146, 170
and Caldwell letter, 147
use of religion as a campaign issue, 154-55, 156
and White, 132
and Mrs. Willebrandt, 176-78, 189-91
Republican National Committee Chairman; *see* Work, Hubert
Republican party, 152, 186
and bigotry, *New York Times* editorial, 148
Klan issue, 32
and prosperity, 2, 111, 119, 120, 126, 148, 195
scandals, 31
White's retraction, 134, 135
Ring kissing, 21, 44, 47-48, 50, 90, 156
Robinson, Edgar Eugene, 120
Robinson, Joseph T.
acceptance speech, 152-53
on Heflin, 82
nomination, 110
Smith's appointments, 152-53
on tolerance, 153
Roosevelt, Franklin D.
1932 candidate, 199
on 1924 convention, 33-34, 72
on Ku Klux Klan, 72
letters from 1924 convention delegates to, 35-38
on Marshall's "Letter," 71-72
on Raskob appointment, 122, 125
on Smith
appointments, 73
church and state, 73
public schools, 73
religion, 66-67
Roosevelt, Theodore, 11, 13-14, 16, 89, 104, 111, 148
"Rum, Romanism and Rebellion," 12-13, 179, 193, 194

Sands, William Franklin, 42-43
Sedgwick, Ellery, 66-67, 69-73, 75, 78
"Sidewalks of New York," 160
"Silent issue," 23; *see also* Religious issue
Simmons, Furnifold McLendel, 158
Smith, Alfred E.
acceptance speech, 125
appointments
Robinson on, 152-53
F. D. Roosevelt on, 73
Smith on, 180-82
James J. Walker, 178-79
Autobiography, 1
business attitude toward, 121-22
church and state, 76, 84
convention, 1924 Democratic, 2, 28, 32-35
Dieffenbach's advice to, 62
drunkenness charges, 127-28, 152, 162
farm problem, 119
governorship, 21-22, 180-82
F. D. Roosevelt on, 72-73
gubernatorial elections, 21-23, 36, 38
"Heavy Load for Al, A," cartoon, 84
Hoover on 1928 defeat of, 151-52
1927 inaugural address, 60, 71
kissing of cardinal's ring, 48
legislative record, 129
F. D. Roosevelt on, 72
White on, 130-31, 133-34
Leonard's charges, 47-51
Liberty League, 116

nomination for president, 2, 100-101, 103-105, 110-12
notification ceremonies, 143-44
Oklahoma City speech, 179-89
on Owen, 182
Papers, 45-47, 119, 179
on parochial schools, 76
political assets, 99, 111, 112
popular vote for, 195
Prohibition, 22, 39, 113, 131
public schools
Robinson on Smith's record, 152
F. D. Roosevelt on Smith's record, 73
Smith on, 76
religion as 1924 factor, 28
on his religion, 1927 statement, 75
on religion as qualification for office, 76
and rural Americans, 57-58
southern states 1928 rejection of, 195
Straton, 136-44
Tammany, 116-17
thoughts on 1928 defeat, 1
vice charges
by Miller, 129
by Straton, 137-41
by White, 130-31
wet telegram, 113-14, 118, 189
White, William Allen
1926 praise of Smith, 129
retraction, 132, 134-35
on Smith's legislative record, 130-31, 133-34
on Smith and Tammany, 131, 133
on Smith and Prohibition, 132
Smith's answer to charges, 135-36
Smith's "Reply," 44, 60, 66-79, 87, 156, 187; *see also* Sedgwick, Ellery
composition of, 73-75
newspaper reaction to, 76-77
Roosevelt's role in exchange, 66-67, 70-73
Snobbery, 116, 117
as campaign issue, 158-62
cartoon, 167
Stoddard, Henry L., 12
Stokes, Anson Phelps, 18
Straton, John Roach, 128-29
background, 136-37
at Oklahoma City, 180, 188
Smith's notification ceremonies, 143-44
vice charges, 137-41
Street, Oliver D., 155-57, 186
Syllabus of Errors, 4-5
Sullivan, Mark
on Walsh as candidate, 95-96

Taft, William Howard, 10, 11, 13, 14, 15, 16, 66
Tammany Hall, 57, 191
and Smith, 116-17
letter to Daniels on, 89
Pickett on, 171
Owen on, 180
denounced by Klan, 27
Walsh not connected with, 92
White on, 131, 133
Testem Benevolentiae, 6-11, 18-19
Thompson, Charles Willis, 136
Tiernan, J. Harry, 29
Tilden, Samuel J., 22
Tom Watson Book Co., 105
Trusteeism, 3
Tumulty, Joseph P., 17, 43

Unitarians; *see Christian Register*
United Presbyterian, 64
Universalists, 64-65
"Unwritten Law," 29, 101-102, 173, 196
Up to Now, An Autobiography, 1

van Dyke, Henry, 153, 173, 188, 189
Vatican, 3, 13, 14, 43, 166
Vatican Council of 1869-1870, 5
Volstead Act, 22, 39; *see also* Eighteenth Amendment

Walker, Hugh K., 173
Walker, James J., 44, 178

Walsh, Frank P., 29
Walsh, Thomas J., 125
  California primary defeat, 96
  Catholicism and availability, 93-95
  contrasted with Smith, 92-93, 99-100
  political liabilities, 96-97
  rejects support as Catholic, 98
  support in South, 98-99, 103
  ticket with Hull suggested, 95
Watson, Tom, 16, 85, 105
W. C. T. U., 158
Werner, Morris R., 117
Whispering campaign, 1, 50, 127, 128, 135, 136, 149, 166, 179
White, Edward Douglas, 53
White, William Allen, 107, 126, 128-36, 159
  1926 praise of Smith, 129
  retraction of charges, 134-35
  on Smith's legistlative record, 130-31, 133-34
  on Smith and Prohibition, 132
  on Smith and Tammany, 131, 133
  Smith's answer to charges, 135-36
White supremacy, 24, 85, 157-58
"Wicked Hospitality," *New York Times* editorial, 34-35
Williams, Michael, 42, 101, 188
Willebrandt, Mrs. Mabel Walker
  appeals to Protestants, 175, 176, 190, 191-92
  Callahan quoted by, 192
  on Catholic roots of Prohibition, 193-94
  cartoon, 177
  charged with using religious issue, 175
  comments on, 178, 186, 189-90
  content of speeches, 175, 191
  denies use of religious issue, 191
  provokes Smith's Oklahoma City speech, 178
  replies to Smith's Oklahoma City speech, 189
  Springfield, O., speech, 176
  status in Coolidge administration, 175
  Work, on her status, 190
Wilson, Woodrow, 11, 16-17, 21, 43, 87, 89, 160
Wishart, Alfred W., 61
Work, Hubert
  answer to Robinson, 152
  on Caldwell letter, 147
  rebuke to Street, 156
  on Willebrandt's speeches, 189-91